Praise for the Memoirs of Jeanne Marie Laskas

GROWING GIRLS

"This thoughtful and gently humorous memoir of motherhood is easy to enjoy." —*Hartford Courant*

"I really enjoyed this book since it was sweet and sentimental yet down-to-earth and real."
—Anne-Marie Nichols, Mother of Many Blogs

"A charming addition for parenting or biographical collections." —*Library Journal*

FIFTY ACRES AND A POODLE

"Anyone who's toyed with the idea of moving to the country should read *Fifty Acres*. It's stunning, witty, sly—a wonderful surprise." —Katherine Russell Rich, author of *The Red Devil*

"Jeanne Marie Laskas is a formidable reporter and one damn fine writer." —*Esquire*

"Truly happy endings are rare, and to read about two extremely likable people making their dreams come (mostly) true means a pleasurable read indeed." —*Newsday*

"Humorous . . . This true-life tale charts a big city girl's transformation to farm gal." —*People*

"Rarely has a city girl transformed herself into a country goddess with such humor." —Rita Mae Brown

"The thinking woman's Erma Bombeck . . . Even the most entrenched urbanite will be charmed by this book."
—Andrea Sachs, Time.com

"For anyone who'd like to chuck it all and move to the country." —*Washington Post*

THE EXACT SAME MOON

"Funny, moving, honest, and hopeful." —*Adoptive Families Magazine*

"Lighthearted [and] fascinating." —*Washington Post*

"Laskas paints a self-portrait of an intelligent and insightful woman." —*Elle*

"Laskas tells the twin stories of her mother's sudden paralysis and her own quest to adopt a baby from China. Serious domestic issues both, they're nonetheless treated with Laskas' sparkling sense of humor." —*Pittsburgh Magazine*

"Here is a parable of the human search for nature's comforting, consoling gifts, and, eventually, for those offered by the journey that being a parent provides—a touching story told lyrically, and a story that offers wisdom for us readers to consider." —Dr. Robert Coles, Pulitzer Prize winner

"The book is terrific. Well, of course it is. Anybody familiar with Jeanne Marie's writing would expect a terrific book. But this is beyond that. This is a long, strong hug; a love letter to love itself; an exploration of everything that is important, and why it's important, and why it's worth remembering that it is. . . . [Laskas] writes with a directness, and a grace, and a keen honesty that few writers, even in their best moments, approach. . . . [*The Exact Same Moon* is] a joy to read . . . and in the process, purely by accident, you just might learn to see your own small world in a slightly brighter shade."
—Wil Hylton, columnist, *GQ*

Also by Jeanne Marie Laskas

THE BALLOON LADY AND OTHER PEOPLE I KNOW

WE REMEMBER:
Women Born at the Turn of the Century
Tell the Stories of Their Lives
in Words and Pictures

FIFTY ACRES AND A POODLE:
A Story of Love, Livestock,
and Finding Myself on a Farm

THE EXACT SAME MOON:
Fifty Acres and a Family

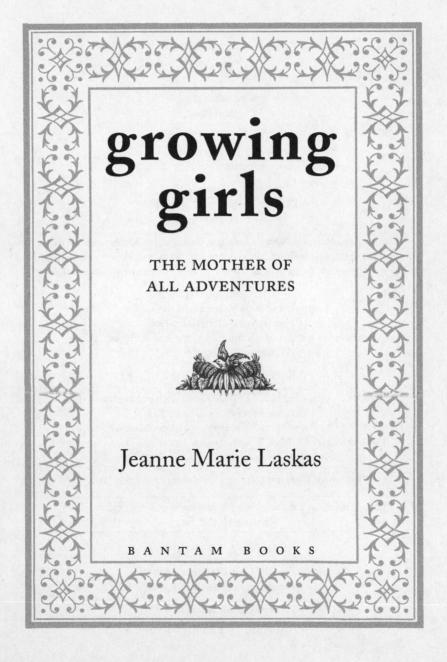

growing girls

THE MOTHER OF ALL ADVENTURES

Jeanne Marie Laskas

BANTAM BOOKS

GROWING GIRLS
A Bantam Book

PUBLISHING HISTORY
Bantam hardcover edition published May 2006
Bantam trade paperback edition / May 2007

Published by Bantam Dell
A Division of Random House, Inc.
New York, New York

This is a work of fiction. Names, characters, places, and incidents either are the
product of the author's imagination or are used fictitiously. Any resemblance
to actual persons, living or dead, events, or locales is entirely coincidental.

For my parents, John and Claire Laskas

*The names and other identifying details
of some characters have been changed
to protect individual privacy.*

contents

bad mother

So much goes on here, yet so little seems to happen.

Steve, one of my cats, stopped eating at some point during our time away. We went east for ten days, visiting my friend Marie at her bright white seashore place in Avalon, then my sister, Claire, in Cherry Hill. At the beach you have that grid pattern of perfectly paved roads, and weed-free lawns made of pebbles, and at Claire's there's a public pool right down the street, a playground across the way, and a cul-de-sac perfect for riding bikes around. I don't think all of New Jersey is this way, but I have to say it was fun being in places where life is so organized and intentional. Out here where we live, on a farm on the side of a Pennsylvania hill, everything is haphazard and shifting. Recently the ground in front of our barn cracked open, revealing a fresh-water spring. This was entirely unprovoked. It was as if the earth just needed a little stretch. Maggie, our mare with bad feet, stood in the cool mud for days and afterwards walked without limping, a miracle.

You would have to see how skinny Steve is to believe it. A bundle of bones beneath his sleek coat of gray and brown. His eyes are a healthy clear green, though. And he started eating again almost as soon as we walked in the door. Now he's lying with me here on the bed, drinking up the companionship. It's sad to think of a cat starving himself with loneliness. It's 3 a.m. and I can't sleep so I decided to just get up and make sense of everything once and for all.

I wrote two books about my life without ever once mentioning Steve because each time I tried to factor him in, his presence made the plot too laborious. Now that is terrible. The idea of just editing one of your cats out of the story of your life. That's terrible!

Lately, whenever I think about myself, it always comes back to this: *bad mother*.

A good mother would have included Steve. A good mother would have bought a house in Cherry Hill with a cul-de-sac for her kids to ride bikes around instead of a place in the middle of nowhere with a rooster.

The rooster was a surprise. Apparently, while we were away, one of our four young so-called hens started to crow. For the record, it sounds nothing like "cockle doodle doo." It's more of an "arrg, arr, arr" that peters out into a kind of cough. The chickens were two days old when we got them. For six weeks they lived in a box in our kitchen, and then we hired Mike, a handsome young carpenter, to build us a chicken coop. One of the things I learned from Mike is that he, too, might be in a feud with George, our neighbor. We only found out that we might be in a feud with George when Gretta, the woman who got us the chickens, intimated as much.

So much goes on here.

Gretta thought the idea of a feud with George was interesting. Gretta grew up in the suburbs, as did I, so she has some distance on the culture I'm just now getting used to. She's years ahead of me on the conversion to country-person, so I regard her as an expert and a model. She's the one who got us our goats, too. Our dogs, Betty and Marley, stay at her place whenever we go away.

Betty is a mutt, or at least she was when I got her over a decade ago. Nowadays you're supposed to say "mix." It's funny to think of politically correct language hitting the dog pound circuit. Marley is a black standard poodle, considerably shaggy thanks to a rough-and-tumble life not suited to his pedigree.

When I went to pick up Betty and Marley at Gretta's house this morning, Betty came charging out and she had an unusually desperate look in her canine eye. Gretta informed me that Betty had had an anxiety attack while we were gone. There was a thunderstorm in the middle of the night; Betty has never been good with storms. I'm usually there to hold her while she shivers. But I wasn't there. Betty dug her way out of the dog room—through wallboard—and got into the garage and dug holes into bottles of the anti-goose chemical Gretta uses in her goose-control business. Three gallons spilled out, at a hundred dollars a gallon, but it was nontoxic so Betty didn't get poisoned.

Even so, when I got home, I felt like a bad mother with a

skinny cat and a dog I wasn't there for during her extreme hour of need. *Bad mother*.

Claire's daughter, Elizabeth, is five, just like my daughter Anna, and she has one of those new Razor scooters with rollerblade wheels on it. She rode this with abandon up and over the Cherry Hill sidewalks and down to the cul-de-sac to visit her neighborhood friends. My girls had never even seen a Razor scooter before, let alone a neighborhood friend, and I had to teach them to stay on the *white* (the sidewalk) and never go on the *black* (the road) unless a grown-up was present. We live on a dirt road and so we have to drive a ways to even get to asphalt.

Anna was adopted from an orphanage in China. She was eleven months old when we got her on a clear February afternoon in a hotel lobby in Nanjing. She was wrapped in a fluffy orange snowsuit decorated with little white cats. I stopped thinking about her birth-mother the same day they drove us by the spot on the street in Kunshan where Anna was found when she was just a few days old. I just couldn't bear to think about that ghost-woman anymore. What good would it do to keep worrying about her and hating her for what she did? "I was born in China," Anna will say. "And then you came to get me." That's right. That's the story. I don't know when to fill in the details.

Sasha, who is three, was fourteen months old when we got her on a sweltering June morning in an office building in Guangzhou. She had on a one-piece playsuit with Mickey Mouse on it and she had the skinniest arms. We never got to see where Sasha was found. We just know she was in a paper box on the steps of a pharmacy. I was already used to blocking out the ghost-women of China, so I put Sasha's birth-mother in that convenient vacuum. Anna and Sasha are strikingly pretty girls, and when they ride together in the supermarket cart, people often comment on this, and then they say, "Are they *real* sisters?" Some adoptive parents get angry with such invasive questions, and some even have curt replies at the ready, but I just say, "Yes," and move on to find the bananas.

Sasha is hardly talking at all yet and a few weeks ago she was diagnosed with verbal apraxia, a neurological disorder that might be the result of minor brain damage in the womb or during infancy, or might be just a dumb coincidence; no one knows.

It was fun visiting Marie at the beach. She and I were best friends in college and she used to sleep at the bottom of my bed like a pet. We love telling this story. "Do you know how many times you've told me that story?" my husband, Alex, will say. Marie got married right out of college and got her MBA and then her PhD while also having her three babies. Her oldest son, Packy, is about to enter his senior year of high school and he's a lifeguard on the beach. He's tan and smart and charming and he plans to go to Harvard or Yale or Penn. In one day Marie's youngest son, ten-year-old Daniel, had a sailing lesson at the yacht club followed by a tennis lesson and then nine holes of golf.

When I told Marie about the chickens in our kitchen, that was when I felt the divide most acutely.

I didn't get married until I was thirty-nine, when everything about my life turned good. We moved to the farm and adopted the girls and gradually our farm in Scenery Hill, Pennsylvania, started filling up with animals. This is a childhood dream I forgot about for half my life. Then Alex entered the picture and I got back to it. Sometimes I worry that he and I are living just *my* dream, and not his. When I get like this I end up surprising him with large motorized vehicles, usually all-wheel-drive. For Father's Day this year I got him one of those motorcycles on four wheels that you can drive up hills and into ditches and get mud splattered all up and down your leg. As I was working out the financing, the guys at the Honda dealership gathered round to see what a woman surprising her husband with an ATV actually . . . looked like. I felt I should have dressed better.

Now it's 3:30 a.m. and I'm no closer to sleep. This has been going on for months now. I'm starting to drink a lot of wine. After I get the girls in bed I have Pinot Grigio and I watch reality TV. Tonight, on the season finale of *For Love or Money*, Preston picked PJ to love, the innocent young thing aching for it. She needed it so bad she decided to pick Preston over a check for a million dollars, which was offered to her if she would just dump Preston. There was so much honor in all of this and so much stupidity. The show gets me very worked up, and I can't sleep.

I don't understand why I'm so lonely. I tell Alex and I can sense he thinks it's some reflection on him, or my love for him, or some lack of love for him, which is completely off base, so I don't even bother telling him anymore.

I wish Gretta lived closer. It takes me forty-five minutes to drive to her house. Out here, that's considered a neighbor. She and I are buddies despite the distance and despite our political divide. Everyone around here is a flag-waving Republican. A lot of people have flag decals on the back windows of their pickups. If you were to say publicly at a bar or at the county fair that you don't think this war we're in is a valid one, you would be accused of not supporting our troops. I don't understand how hoping that pimply young men and beautiful young women don't die in the line of enemy fire has anything whatsoever to do with political views. I support our troops in that I just want them all to come home to their moms and have pie.

Politically, I tried for years to be "Independent," to lean neither all the way left nor right. But like everyone else, I seem to be getting narrow and cranky and one-sided. The part that enrages me most is all the yanking in the name of God. The God I know is exhausted, sick in bed with an ice bag on His head. The God I know isn't some authoritarian dictator with a rule book written in especially cryptic prose able to be deciphered by only one chosen group. The God I know is creative and hilarious and humble and constantly revising. Right about now He's wishing America would pipe down and bow off the world stage for a while and get a good nap and then, with a fresh head, reconsider just about everything.

I think about this business a lot when I watch our goats and our little donkey try to share a feed bowl. Just because the goats are the aggressive eaters and bully their way in doesn't mean someone shouldn't pull the timid donkey aside and make sure she gets lunch. The God I know finds these matters of utmost importance.

You talk like that at a bar or at the county fair and at best someone is going to smile at you like you're a child, but most likely just interrupt you and remind you that, hey, God says gay people shouldn't get married.

The last time I was visiting my family in Philadelphia, all of whom have swung in the opposite direction of me politically, I said I was starting a new party called the Hypocrites, a group that believed in telling the truth only when it would offer immediate personal gain. "I'm a Hypocrite!" I said. "I think it can really catch on."

My mother is so feeble now. She's eighty-two and I don't think there is any way she can come visit me here at the farm. If the six-hour drive doesn't do her in, the rough terrain will. She's "recovered" from the strange paralyzing disease she contracted over five years ago, but she's not the same. She came to Claire's house for lunch, and just watching the kids bounce around exhausted her. Then she tripped over a throw rug. I heard the thud and I ran in and Alex ran after me and between the two of us we got my mother upright in no time. But we promised not to tell my father. To her credit, my mother blamed the throw rug.

I'm writing these thoughts on the back of drawings my girls did earlier today while I was cooking corn. They ran in with scribbles, performances they wanted me to hang up. Eventually they decided to leave me out of the equation and they just went ahead and grabbed the tape. The walls of this house are now covered with my daughters' drawings.

I don't think Claire had a single drawing on her walls. Her house is so much neater than mine. I think it's because she has a utility room. Claire is two years older than me. She's a pediatrician and she tells me not to be overly concerned about Sasha's speech, but I can see the worry in her eyes. When she redid her kitchen last year she got refrigerator doors that match her cabinets. Meaning: wood. Meaning: nothing to hang stuff on with magnets. I don't fully understand this decision.

My girls hang ponies on our refrigerator. Ponies are the

biggest thing going. My Little Pony, a Hasbro toy. They're kind of like the Barbie dolls of the animal world. They come in pink and purple and yellow and blue and white with hair that is long and sparkly and sometimes rainbow. They all have big blue eyes and identical expressions and one hoof that is secretly a magnet. The magnet is responsible for all the magic. Wave the pony over the door of her magic dressing room and a song plays and lights flash. That's fun. But my girls figured out that the magnet also means the ponies will hang on the refrigerator. We now have ponies hanging all over ours, sticking out, perpendicular, hair blowing in the air conditioner breeze.

Naturally, when Sasha ran to Claire's refrigerator and stuck her pony on it, it fell with a thud to the floor. "Hey!" my daughter said, angrily. *"Hey!"*

Right now I'm in Anna's bed, in her room, because it's cool and she isn't here to kick me in the head or in the liver. She got out of her bed and came to mine and Alex's because of a bad dream. We have a king-sized bed for expressly this purpose, a place for kids to crawl in if need be. But Anna kicks, so usually I leave.

Her room has drawings of ponies all over it. She draws them and then names them: Catt Sweet, Butterfly Summer Candy, Popsicle Rose Bush, Moonlight Dream.

I'm scanning the walls with all these drawings and all these made-up names, and I am wondering what sort of fairy tales go on in my little girl's head.

So much goes on here.

Tomorrow I'm going to be a wreck because I'm not sleeping. I have to prune. The thing about farm life is, so very much cutting goes on. All the weeds coming and going. The redistribution of vegetation. I was thinking about this while I was outside with the girls, and then I looked up and faced the fact that one of our Norway spruce trees really is dead. The agony I felt for that tree sent me spiraling. Did I pay enough attention to it during its life? Did I sit under it and get a good feel for its shade and its particular aroma?

And what, then, of my daylilies? I wonder if I'm making enough fuss over them. Just because a flower is in bloom, does that mean you have to keep visiting it? How much visiting is enough? And if I don't save the primroses from getting choked by the morning glory vine, does this make me bad?

Everything keeps coming back to this: *bad mother.*

My mother often says she was a bad mother. When I was six months old, her parents came to live in an apartment in our basement and then her dad died and then her mom went senile. "You can just wipe the entire decade of my forties out of my life!" she'll say, and then she'll turn to me, recognizing that that wipes me out. She apologizes for not being there.

I am aware of no infractions whatsoever; I think of her only as a good mother.

What's funny is that I never think of myself as a bad daughter. And yet I was so mischievous. I was a naughty, naughty daughter who never got caught because my mother was so busy with all she had going on. So, why don't I carry "Bad daughter!" around instead of "Bad mother!" when I think of myself? It's funny but this is simply not the way it works. Probably if you were able to listen in to the contents of women's minds, you would hear a lot of them saying "Bad mother!" to themselves.

When Mike built the chicken coop, he was supposed to put

a little hinged door on one side with a ramp off it so the chickens could walk outside and do their pecking. Then we were going to enclose the whole little chicken yard with chicken wire to keep the raccoons out. But Mike ran out of time before he got the door made. He said he would be back in July. Meantime the chickens live inside the coop and the only time they come out is when we let them out and sit there with them. Other than that, it's an indoor life. Can you believe I wake up worrying about this? I worry that my chickens are missing out on worms and grubs. Then I think I better call Mike and nag before it's too late and my chickens get some kind of disorder like kids who watch too much TV. The amount of time I spend thinking about this takes away from time I could be worrying about whether or not our mule Skippy needs his hooves trimmed and if I had spent more quality time with Greg, our goat, when he was a baby maybe he wouldn't buck me in the head when I bend over to pick up his food bowl. *Bad mother!*

If this weren't me I was talking to, I would say, "Relax." And: "Don't you understand?" Feeling like a bad mother is the only way to be a mother. Motherhood begins with worry. This is the first thing you have to have, and if you have a lot it just means you're big enough to carry it.

I think loneliness is an occupational hazard of motherhood. And by motherhood I mean the job of any caretaker. Being in charge of the mental health of four chickens means you don't get to be a chicken.

"Freedom isn't free!" said a sign on the way to Gretta's. And then I saw another sign down the road saying yes to Jesus. I'm glad Gretta doesn't have signs on her lawn.

Oh, and one more thing. I'm a bad mother. Sasha tells me this whenever I correct her with even a tiny dose of authority. "Bat!" she yells, which is how she pronounces "bad." "Bat! Bat! *Bat!*" She of so few words.

If I were a good mother, Anna would have more friends. She would have neighborhood friends to ride scooters with. This is what I want for her. It's funny I worry about her more than I worry about Sasha. With so little language, Sasha communicates so much already. Anna is internal. She doesn't even *want* friends. She has Sasha and she has her ponies.

Sometime during the summer of 2001, when we brought Sasha home, Alex woke up in the middle of the night and noticed blood everywhere. "I need help!" he began saying, through gasps of air. When I saw the blood, I figured he'd been shot. I had no idea who would want to shoot my husband. He was sweating and saying, "Help!" I called 911 and helped him get to the bathroom because the blood was pouring out of his rectum. The EMT guys got right to work, sticking needles in him and strapping him onto the cot, and I tried to be calm but as they wheeled him over the patio I felt a duty to tell them that they'd neglected to take his blood pressure. "When you can't feel a pulse, you're not so much worried about the number," one said. The last thing I saw was Alex's white feet as they closed the ambulance door. "Um, will someone call me or something?" I said to the driver. Anna and Sasha had, remarkably, slept through the ordeal and I cleaned and scrubbed up all the blood before they awoke to see it. It was something to do while I waited to hear if my husband was still alive.

The EMT guys, it turned out, saved his life. Without their

intervention, Alex would have "bled out," as they say on crime shows. A few days earlier Alex had gotten a routine colonoscopy and a tiny polyp was removed. This resulted in a scab somewhere in his large intestine. When the scab sloughed itself off, it let open the floodgates. This probably wouldn't have happened if someone had told him to stop taking the ibuprofen he uses to control headaches. But no one did. The ibuprofen thinned his blood and he nearly bled out.

Later on I wrote about this in a magazine article, more as a way of fulfilling a contractual obligation with the magazine—and as a public service to anyone getting a colonoscopy, and as a way of venting my outrage at the people who never told him to stop the ibuprofen—than as a chance to make the business of my husband's rectum public. That part was a little hard to negotiate. In the story, I said something about what it was like to live out in the middle of nowhere at 3 a.m. when you've just witnessed an ambulance door closing on your husband's white feet. I wrote about how I sat there and in my shock I couldn't think of what to do, other than clean up his blood. I wrote about how I felt it would have been *rude* to call anyone before the sun came up. I have no idea how I came to this conclusion. Who understands the workings of the brain under normal circumstances, let alone during a time when you're terrified your husband is dead? Anyway, in the magazine article, I wrote about how I figured I had to wait until 6 a.m. before I could call anyone, and how at six I called my friends Wendy and Gretta and they both took the girls so I could join Alex in the ICU.

Our neighbor George and his wife, Pat, saw the story in the magazine, and Pat was upset. "You could have called me!" she said. "You could have called me at 3 a.m. and I would have come right over." She was right. I know she would have. I have no idea why I didn't think to call her.

Then I didn't hear from her for a while. And George didn't put sheep on our fields like he used to. And he didn't plant alfalfa on our one field or oats that we would split with him. And the following spring they didn't invite us over to see the sea of baby lambs frolicking.

So then, just a few weeks ago, Gretta drove with George to a sheep disease conference. They got to talking about us. This was nearly two years after Alex nearly bled out on a hot summer night. George told Gretta that Pat had been quite upset that I said, publicly, and to a national audience, that country people were the types of people you can't call at 3 a.m. if you need help.

But—this was a story about Alex almost *dying*, not about George and Pat.

But!

And so began the feud we've been having, which I didn't actually know we were having, and I am not entirely certain we *are* having, with our neighbors for nearly two years.

So much goes on here and yet so little seems to happen.

At speech therapy this morning, Miss Sandy tried to get Sasha to say "apple." She could say "ap" and "pull" as clear as day. Ap. Pull. Ap. Pull. But when she tried to put them together it kept coming out "apap."

birthday chicken

The story of Birthday, the chicken that ran backwards in circles, began on my daughter Anna's fifth birthday. This was our virgin voyage into the chicken world, and easily enough we got sold on the virtues of "silkie bantams," a breed known as being fancy. "I'm telling you, these are the poodles of the chicken world!" the woman at the feed store said, intending this as a selling point.

It wasn't, actually, the fancy part that attracted me to silkies. My heart did not go aflutter at the thought of a fluffy chicken with feathers extending clear down its legs and onward to its toes, which, I learned, number five instead of the more typically chicken four, and are black instead of the more typically chicken orange. Also, silkies have blue earlobes. According to the American Silkie Bantam Club, certainly their most devoted fans, these "beguiling oddities" have charmed people for centuries, most notably Marco Polo, who wrote of them during his journeys to China in the thirteenth century.

And good for him. As for me, I was drawn to the fact that silkies are said to be docile, far more so than your average chicken; with relative ease they will befriend your kids and turn themselves into pets.

So for her fifth birthday, Anna was presented with the gift of four silkie bantam peeps. They were the size of golf balls, two white and two "blue," a term farm people prefer to the word "gray" whether you are talking chickens or horses or goats. We kept the peeps in a box in our kitchen, and soon enough I made up a list of chicken rules and stuck it on the refrigerator. BE GENTLE. YOU MUST BE SEATED ON THE FLOOR IF YOU WANT TO HOLD CHICKENS. NO RUNNING WITH CHICKENS. DO NOT DROP CHICKENS. DO NOT CARRY CHICKENS ON YOUR HEAD OR ON YOUR SHOULDERS. IF YOU PUT CHICKENS IN DOLL-HOUSE DO NOT COVER THEM WITH BLANKETS OR LOCK IN LIT-TLE OVEN. OR LITTLE TOY BOX. OR LITTLE CLOSET. The list kept getting longer as the chickens grew and the girls could squish them into only increasingly larger enclosures, a kind of a blessing.

Anna named the chickens: Birthday, Mary, Marie, and Shintzee.

"Shintzee?" I said.

"No, Shan-cee," she said.

"Shan-cee?"

"No, Mommy, Chaun-tee."

This conversation happens every time. I have no idea what that chicken's name is.

Birthday's condition came on suddenly enough. One day we looked in the box and one of the gray chicks looked exactly like what you picture when you say, "She was running like a chicken with her head cut off."

Her head appeared to be missing. She was just a little feather ball, scooting backwards, around and around and around.

Anna, who already had emerged the best chicken handler of the family by a very long shot, reached in and picked the crazy chicken up. She looked underneath her. "It's here!" she said. She eased the neck straight and there it was, right where it belonged: Birthday's head. Birthday looked around, shook that head, and seemed, at that moment, to be back with us. "Well, good," we all said.

But the next time we looked in the box, there was Birthday, headless and scooting backwards again. The other chicks didn't seem even a little interested in this apparent fit, except when she bumped into them, and they would simply bump back. The condition did not stop Birthday from eating or drinking or growing, but it was, by anyone's reckoning, creepy.

"You ever heard of a chicken tucking its head under and running backwards?" I said to Dr. Hurley, our vet. I Googled. I could find no information whatsoever on why a little chick might get stuck in spasms of this or any other sort.

We decided Birthday would grow out of it, kind of like a baby with colic, and every day we hoped, as we got on with our new life as chicken people.

"We have to get them out of the kitchen," I said to Alex. "We must not become people with chickens in our kitchen."

"We *are* people with chickens in our kitchen," he said.

"We must stop," I said.

We moved the chickens into the living room. The March winds had not died down; it was still too cold for outdoor peep survival. And they were so small and defenseless against our dogs and cats, some of which actually drooled while looking upon them. The worst offender was Marley. It seemed especially insidious to me that a poodle would have dining designs on the poodles of the chicken world.

One morning Anna found Elmo, our orange cat, standing on top of the little chicken box, reaching in. She shouted and scared him off and right then and there her bond with the chickens grew stronger. "Did I save the day?" she said. "Am I the hero?" I told her yes, and yes, and yes, and tried not to worry about her need for validation.

As for Birthday, she scooted backwards and backwards and backwards for nearly a whole day after the Elmo incident. We came to understand the chick's condition as one of nerves, the spasms most acute during times of stress. Each time, you had to pick her up, ease her neck straight. And each time, from the way she'd shake her head, it seemed she was thankful for the help. "Whew. Thanks. I just couldn't get it together there. . . ."

Soon enough, as Birthday emerged a full-grown hen, we decided she had a rare neurological disorder like epilepsy that would perhaps affect the quality of her life only in spurts, and this was just who she was. *"Is that chicken okay?!"* people visiting our house would say, horrified by the display of chicken seizures. And maybe, by simply getting used to it, we became indoctrinated into our new world as chicken people in a full and profound way. Sort of like when you see people at restaurants dining with relatives who have tubes up their noses. These people just go about eating their pork chops, paying no mind to the fact that one of their own is attached to an oxygen tank. At some point they crossed the barrier from these people to *those* people, so fully and completely that they'd forgotten all about it.

This is the kind of chicken people we became. People with chickens in our living room who without fanfare turned into people with chickens living outside in a brand-new chicken coop under the Norway maple. This turned out to be a perfect place for a chicken coop because there was already a picnic table there and so we had a place to sit and watch as they entertained us with their pecking and squawking.

Now, *brooder* is an interesting word. People who worry a lot in silence are known as brooders. But then again so is a hen sitting on her eggs. The more I get to know chickens, the more I realize half our language comes from chickens. Well, not half. But an awful lot considering this isn't Latin or anything. Cooped up. Egghead. Hatch a plan. Henpecked. Pecker. Cock. Chickenshit. Chicken-scratch. A lot of chicken words are meant to deliver attitude, which isn't surprising to me now that I have chickens. Chickens aren't background animals like fish or sheep or horses. Chickens are in-your-face animals. Chickens, if you have them, come to bracket your days. The rooster hollers all morning, and then in the evening the hens have left you their mysterious gift of eggs.

Silkies are said to be excellent brooders, to have a tendency toward "broodiness." This, too, is usually meant as a compliment.

Once a silkie hen has decided to set on her eggs, there is very little that will bring her from the nest until those eggs have hatched. Apparently, other breeds of chickens get distracted, or disinterested, or maybe just impatient. But a silkie won't give up. In fact, a silkie hen will hatch and raise most any kind of poultry or game fowl. Many breeders of quail or pheasant who prefer to hatch naturally as opposed to in an incubator will keep a flock of silkie hens for this purpose. A hen that begins to set is said to have "gone broody."

I never knew I had an opinion on such matters, but when I learned that silkies were broody, I started loving them. It opened my heart. Sort of like, "Good girl, sitting on your eggs like that!" Here were chickens that inherently understood the sacrifices of motherhood, chickens I could look up to. Wouldn't, after all, that mama hen rather be out with the boys pecking on the ground for worms and aphids and centipedes? Wouldn't she? Instead, silkies had a higher calling. Here were chickens who stayed home and brooded.

The women of my mother's generation stayed home and brooded. The women of my generation got trained out of that value system and were taught to be courageous enough to go out and peck with the big boys. Saying that someone is hen-pecked nowadays would be more of an insult to the offending female, who surely has better things to do with her time, than it would be to the subordinate male, who, anyway, has enough to worry about trying to figure out what happened to his almighty cock.

Chicken language, I'm telling you, is everywhere. The average person probably can't get through a day without having a thought that has some long-lost connection to a chicken.

Anna's connection was far more literal. Her first summer with chickens was indeed an all-chicken summer. She would sit for hours after dinner, while I gardened and Sasha dug for worms. Anna's bond with those chickens made my heart leap. Soon I even stopped questioning her judgment as she went about selecting which chicken to put in the bucket of honor. The chicken would fit in that bucket as if in a little nest, only it couldn't move because the feet didn't quite reach the bottom. It would just sit there going "bawk bawk," as a chicken does, while Anna looked at it. Eventually, she would curl up on the picnic table next to it, and tell it stories of the stars or the moon or show the chicken how her tongue had turned green on account of an ice pop.

Naturally, since she was the easiest to catch, Birthday became the chicken most likely to be placed in the bucket of honor, and so you could say she became Anna's favorite.

Summer probably always does this, but summer slowed me down. I was supposed to write a book about being a mom, to organize my thoughts into chapters and figure out a structure to hang them on, to make a lasting point, but somehow I decided to go ahead and become a mother instead.

Brooding is more something I do when I'm working. I know so much more about sitting around worrying about a work project than I do about worrying about kids. This could just be a fact of life for older moms. We've worked and worked and worked and if we are lucky enough to finally have a child or two, we find ourselves suddenly catapulted into a most alien kind of chaos.

Work is so much easier. Anyone will tell you that. To have a desk, where you have everything all lined up, and a schedule you more or less get to agree to. Work. I am a worker. This is so funny because I never really think of my work as work. I certainly never thought of myself as having a career. Writing, work, this is just who I am. I am a person who sits at a desk and makes phone calls and taps at a computer keyboard and sips coffee and calls her mom at five. That I am anything bigger or smaller than that has come as sudden news to me.

Brand new.

News.

And now I find that this, too, is a cliché, that women my age all across the land know this one. Bankers and lawyers and scientists. I always figured those people had themselves bracketed. They picked real careers. They picked office jobs. They picked out suits and they took trains to tall buildings. I thought they knew what they were doing, whereas I was just sort of a drifter. They made choices. Career first, then husband, then kids. Or a different sequence depending on how things best added up. The point is, they chose to be workers or wives or mothers, whereas I actually had no choice. I had one thing I knew how to do and I had to pay the bills, so I did it. Then I started liking it, then I started loving it, and then I realized it was: me. The rest of the picture? The husband, the children? Oh, well. You can't force one kind of love over another, just because you think it would be your preference.

You read in newspapers and newsmagazines about women nowadays who were so busy with careers they never had time to forge relationships and now there's no ticking or tocking left on the biological clock. This is usually leveled as a sort of criticism. These women were either foolish or self-indulgent or both. Too bad, ladies. You should have stuck with the way it was in the old days, back when women just stayed home and brooded.

It's easy for any sad woman to buy into this. I bought into it when I was in a mood to feel sorry for myself. But then I forgave myself because I was a drifter. I was just doing what I was good at, while waiting for love. I was developing the one part of me that at least vaguely seemed worth developing. I didn't completely *care* about me, or my mind, or my talents—did that somehow vindicate me for putting off motherhood?

I wonder why it's easier for me to diminish myself than it is for me to admit that I am a woman who quite vigorously forged a career. Stuck so far back in our minds, all the way back to a place that precedes even chicken language, is the notion that the brooders are the superior class of our gender.

Of course I was forging a career. Of course I was making choices, every bit as much as the banker and the lawyer and the scientist. And of course those women were drifting, every bit as much as I was. Isn't there a higher vantage point here? Some hilltop where we can see that the brooder and the seeker, we are all just doing what we do, and the best we can hope is that we're brave enough to do our best? That's the spiritual quest. To say women should heed one call versus another lest they lose out on biological matters is to lose touch with the Divine.

One thing I know: I would have been a terrible mom back in my twenties and thirties, when I was all broody with my stories. It took me until I was thirty-nine to be ready, and by then my ovaries were having none of it. People are perhaps the only species with brains enough to find the idea of adoption somewhat suspect. When I look around our farm, at a goat raising a lamb, at a chicken perfectly willing to hatch a quail or an ostrich, I fall back at ease once again with the notion that a mom is a mom is a mom.

The women in China who hatched Anna and Sasha weren't ready to brood, or weren't allowed to brood, or for some other reason the timing in those nests was off. Here is my nest. Here is my time. Here is all this love I've been storing up. Even the dumbest fat hen in the world sooner or later answers nature's call to give.

One of the things that happens when you let go and allow yourself to be a mom is you see your children from different angles and discover richness. This happened in our kiddie pool, where I spent a good part of the summer not writing and trying my best not to care about it. It was a pool big enough for three and deep enough for throwing. I would toss Sasha up in the air and listen to a whole new laugh as she splashed. She sounded like a little bell. We got a SpongeBob raft and Anna rode on it while I pushed, and I discovered that up close her head smells exactly like Tetley tea.

In the end, Birthday never did grow out of her condition. The longer we waited, the more we came to conclude that she had a rare disease that would probably end her life prematurely but, for now, she was more or less thriving.

We had bigger chicken worries. Shortly after our chicks differentiated without doubt into two roosters (Marie and Shintzee or Chauntee or Shancee) and two hens (Mary and Birthday), one of the roosters tore after Anna and started pecking her feet.

This was a shame on so many levels. These were Anna's first real babies. This was her first trial period at being a mom. And for a five-year-old with a crazy backwards-running chicken, she'd done an excellent job. These were the creatures she had nursed along into adulthood, or at least adolescence. I guess it would be like any parent with a teenager who goes off and turns into a neo-Nazi. Because this rooster, which for the sake of ease we will just once and for all call Shintzee, was not simply having a bad afternoon. Nor could the pecking be written off as a mistake. That rooster darted after Anna as she approached the maple tree in her usual way until pretty soon she was way up at the dahlia bed screaming, "Ack! Ack! Ack! He's pecking! He's Bad! BAD BAD BAD BAD!" And when I finally kicked the rooster away and brought Anna into my arms, I could see little red dots on her feet.

It was a hard one to spin. Anna's such a fearful child. And here was a trusted friend turning on her. Would her relationship to chickens be forever severed?

"It's okay, sweetie, I have you," I said. "I have you. That rooster is cranky!"

"Why is he cranky?" she asked, sobbing. "Why? Why? Why?"

Um. I knew nothing of chicken moods. "Everyone gets cranky," I said. "But that's never a reason to hurt someone. That rooster was wrong."

It seemed like a good enough time to reinforce the lesson of not hitting or pinching just because one happens to feel like it.

But I had more work to do. The last thing I wanted was for her to lose chickens from her life, or for her to have her summer of chicken love end like this. So I convinced her. I convinced her this was surely a one-time thing, that she should go on back down to the maple tree the next day and pay that rooster no mind.

She believed me. The next morning she went down to say good morning to the chickens. I stayed up at the house, hoping not to make a big deal of any of this. Next thing I hear: "Ack! Ack! Ack! He's Bad! BAD BAD BAD BAD!" And there was Anna up by the dahlia bed again, in tears.

This was a shame on so very many levels.

I called Gretta. "Our rooster has started pecking my children," I told her.

"Oh," she said. "Well, you have to get rid of it."

Just like that?

"Some of them have it in them. Once they peck, they'll always peck. It only happens with the males. You have to get rid of it."

For an instant I feared that Gretta was going to advise shooting the rooster, perhaps even boiling it for dinner.

"I'll take him," she said. She had six other roosters. "Once he gets here, my boys will show him how to act."

She offered to give us three hens in exchange. She said she was needing to let go of her hens anyway. Her husband is allergic to eggs. No one else lives at their house. "I can't eat all these eggs."

And so one morning I put Shintzee very carefully in an empty case of Amstel Light and we met Gretta up at the church with the big green roof where Sasha gets her speech therapy, a convenient halfway point between my farm and Gretta's. Sasha was in there trying to say words that end in "n." Moon. Tune. Loon. Phone. Bone. Stone. And all of them came out ending in a "d" sound, mood, tude, lood, phode, bode, stode, while Anna and I waited in the parking lot for Gretta. We said our goodbyes to Shintzee and talked about forgiveness. Anna did not seem upset to lose the rooster.

"He's a pecky one, Mommy," she said, disapprovingly. "A pecky one."

"Yes, he is, sweetie." It seemed, at that moment, to be the girls against the boys, and we girls had that boy trapped in a cardboard beer box.

Yay, us. It's funny to look at how often the battles at the farm play out this way. Living on a farm proves all the worst things about men. The fact of the matter is that most males of most farm animals are either slaughtered or neutered. This is no accident. Look at sheep. All those sheep you see dotting all those hills? Ewes. Farmers keep the ewes because they have babies, increasing the flock, and because they are docile and never ever give anyone a single problem. A ram is something you keep somewhere else, off in another pasture with, perhaps, a male of another species to keep it company, and a very, very strong fence. That male will do whatever it can to get to those ewes, which is nothing compared to what a jackass, or male donkey, will do to get to a jenny, its female counterpart. I once visited a farm with a jackass and the poor crazed creature was like a bad actor playing a most unconvincing jailed convict. Surely no creature snorts this violently, this continuously, this crazily, for this long. *Hee haw hee haw hee haw!* Then: *bam!*— the sound of the animal throwing itself against the barn stall, which had been reinforced with iron rods. It seems to me that any time I have ever visited any farm and been introduced to the male of any species—"and this is our bull," "and this is our buck," "and this is our ram"—I am also introduced to a fantastic construction project to keep that animal contained.

One day at a llama farm I saw Bruno, the sire, get so upset by the sight of a skunk about to enter his girl-llama's pasture that he tore after it and in one swift motion stomped it to death.

For the record, like a lot of women I don't have a husband who snorts or head-butts or stomps skunks or behaves in ways instantly recognizable in the ram or the buck or the bull or the sire. My husband makes his living as a very calm, compassionate psychotherapist. But in the gender as a whole, and certainly in the NFL, the snorting farm animal can be readily seen.

One more disclaimer: horses. Females are known to be difficult, nervous, "spooky," temperamental, whereas geldings are easygoing and relatively calm. It is important to note, though, that a gelding is a neutered male; this seems to be the key to everything.

So Shintzee the pecky rooster waited in the beer box and Anna and I stood by as Gretta drove up. She got out and opened her hatchback and inside there were the three hens in a cage. A tan one, black one, and a speckled gray one. In short order Anna named them Penelope, Magenta, and Hollyhock.

Then, right there in Gretta's hatchback, Penelope laid an egg.

It was our first official egg.

I was appalled. An egg? Really? I felt embarrassed for Penelope. Wasn't this something a hen did in . . . private? Expelling items from one's body seemed to me as if it should be a behind-the-scenes thing.

"An egg!" I said to Gretta.

She picked it up, handed it to Anna, who offered her scared smile, a downward twist of the lips.

"Aigg! Aigg! Aigg!" Sasha said when she came out with Sandy, the speech therapist, who was trying to figure out what was going on.

We said goodbye to our pecky rooster and never looked back.

So now I'm supposed to come to the happily-ever-after part of the story of Birthday, the chicken that ran backwards in circles. But of course these sorts of stories never end that way. My only consoling point is that it wasn't Marley who did the deed, but rather one of his visiting friends, a mutt we'll call Sam. (In her shame, Sam's owner has refused to allow her or her dog's identity to be revealed.) We were all watching. We always watch whenever there's a visiting dog. So who knows how it happened. We were out in the garden. How long had we turned our backs?

I saw chicken feathers up by the dahlia bed. A lot of them. Then I saw Sam nosing her kill.

I hated her.

I hated myself. I should have known that poor spastic chicken was an easy catch. I should have taken special measures to protect our special-needs chicken. The others had scurried under the fence, out of harm's way. I can only imagine what the sight of a dog's teeth would have done to Birthday's nervous constitution.

I felt responsible in every way, as mothers are prone to. And so goes the history of the world. You can be the kind of mother who surprises her child with the gift of baby chicks, who puts up with chickens in the kitchen and in the living room, who devotes herself to teaching all the lessons a pecky rooster might have to teach, who in fact provides burial services for all dead pets, and you'll stand there with that dead pet thinking of none of this. Instead you will drown in your failed responsibility. It will be your fault that the crazy chicken got crazy in the first place; you probably permitted too rigorous handling in the dollhouse; you should have put more stringent rules up on the fridge. JUST DON'T TOUCH THE DARN CHICKENS! Then the chicken wouldn't have gotten the nervous condition and wouldn't have gone into those spasms and when the dog came she would have had a running start. *You! You. You call yourself a mother.*

But, exactly.

Alex and I put Birthday's remains in a shoe box and then we got a shovel and we told Anna and Sasha it was time once again to go to the magic tree, a large apple tree on our hill that has become our little pet cemetery. The girls know the drill. They are so good with death.

Anna wanted to open the box so that she could say goodbye to Birthday.

She opened it and did not flinch. "Well, goodbye," she said. "I love you. You were a great chicken. I'm sorry if I didn't protect you but I meant to."

I stepped forward as if to stop her from going where she was going, headlong into guilt and responsibility, but Alex stopped me. He said let her speak. She again apologized to the chicken and then she asked the chicken to check on Buddy, our dead goat, and all of our dead fish and three dead cats and then we walked back down the hill.

It was hot, or maybe my head was just getting hot with the thought of what was next and what just happened. I was wiping my eyes, trying to get a grip. A friend of a friend of Alex's was coming over to clean out our basement of baby gear and baby toys we no longer needed. She was about to become a mom and I was already deep in the trenches. I was trying to figure out how to explain to this woman I hardly knew that I was crying over a dead chicken, but not exactly, and I thought about sitting her down and saying, "You have no idea what you're getting into."

up for grabs

A father, a daughter, a balloon. They are just now heading toward the car, hand in hand, toddling down the driveway. It is the same way every week. They're going to the grocery store. They'll get a free sample of cheese, they'll get a free cookie, she'll ride in the cart awhile, then get down and push. He'll say, "Whose little girl are you?" She'll say, "Daddy's!"

It is the same way every single week. Except there isn't always a balloon.

Alex is an older dad, well into his fifties. Before Anna arrived, he wondered if he could do it. He wondered if he'd have what it takes.

On this day she's barely three. She knows she has an older dad. "I think," she'll say, "he might be twelve."

The balloon is two days old, practically ancient in the life of a standard-issue balloon. It is red. It's tied to the end of a purple ribbon. It has fewer thoughts than a household pet, and yet, to a three-year-old, it is in every way a pet. You have to take care of it, and it won't last forever. But for the time being it is all yours.

The center of everything.

"Would you like me to tie the balloon around your wrist?" Alex is saying, already knowing the answer.

"I would like to hold it," Anna answers. "I would like to hold my balloon in my hand."

"Okay, sweetie," he says. "Well, hold on tight."

The balloon has lost a good bit of its helium, and there is no wind, and so the balloon appears to be walking one step behind her, at just her height. A pal if ever there was one.

He is boosting her up into the car seat, they are fumbling with sleeves, straps, buckles. It's hard to tell how it happens. A slow-motion replay probably could not verify the sequence of events. But the balloon! The balloon gets loose. The balloon is floating in the air, just above the father's head. "Oh, no!" she is saying. "Oh . . . no!" He reaches into the air, tries to pluck it from the sky, but the balloon at that moment catches an updraft and lifts higher, just beyond his grasp.

"Daddy!" she is saying. "Oh, no!"

He tries again; this time he leaps. But the balloon soars a foot higher, hangs there stupidly.

"My balloon," she cries, craning her neck so as to make a more direct appeal. "Please, balloon! Please, Daddy! Oh, my balloon . . ."

Another father might say, "I told you, honey, I told you to

hold on tight!" Another might think, *We have to hurry, we have a long list of groceries.* Another might think, *We can just buy another balloon at the store.*

"That's my balloon!" she is saying, looking into the sky with longing. "That is my best balloon. . . ."

This is one way a father, old or young, finds out who he is, with no time to decide which one he should be, which one he wants to be, which one might, perhaps, look better. When a balloon is loose, there is no time. You either charge after it, or you don't.

And so he finds that he is the kind of man who charges after a loose balloon, charges after it with courage and fight. He isn't aware of his heroism, or his foolishness, he is too busy chasing a balloon. He hops, runs, reaches, trots over the grass and trips into the boxwoods. That balloon is either dancing or flirting or maybe a little of both. It doesn't have enough loft to go into the clouds—no, it hovers, dragging its purple ribbon just beyond his pleading fingertips.

"Get it, Daddy!" she is saying, cheering him on. "Oh, good job, Daddy!"

It is all he needs to hear. It is fuel. He leaps a few more times until he gets an idea. He's going to outsmart that balloon. He calculates its direction, like a receiver estimating the trajectory of a touchdown pass, and he runs past it, up a little hill, to the top of a wall, off of which he can hurl himself and go for the grab.

One, two, three—the timing here is critical—and he leaps! And don't you know that darn balloon darts left. *Left?* The balloon is now over the wall, high in the air.

To another father, that balloon would be a goner for sure. But not him. Not yet. He watches it. He shakes his head. He wonders how he might break the news to her. He thinks, *Life isn't fair.*

Just then the first real breeze of the day kicks in, and the balloon makes a U-turn, an absolute about-face. It drifts toward him, closer now, and closer. He hops at just the right moment. He feels the ribbon like a tickle between his fingers and so he grabs, he grabs happiness out of the sky.

"Aaaah!" she says, her mouth dropping open. "You did it! Daddy did it!" She can't quite believe it's true. Her father has performed a miracle. Her balloon is back. And life, to her, but also to him, has plenty more fairness left.

meeting the ghost-mother

When we were waiting to travel to China to adopt Sasha, I signed up for a Yahoo! group for people who had adopted or were adopting from the Huazhou Social Welfare Institute in Guangdong province, the orphanage in southern China where Sasha was living. The people at the orphanage knew her by the name they'd assigned to her—Ji Hong Bin—if they knew her at all, but Alex and I had already decided to name her Sasha Marie as soon as we got her home. We picked Sasha because it means "little Alex" in Russian and we loved the sound of it. At first I worried that a Russian name for a girl of Chinese ancestry would be somehow . . . crooked. But the truth of the matter was this girl from China was going to be the daughter of a Russian-Lithuanian Jew and a French-Irish-Lithuanian Catholic, so I figured we may as well just go ahead and enjoy the benefits of being a family of mutts, one of which surely must be you aren't beholden to any particular rules of pedigree.

At that point all we had of Sasha was a little picture, her date of birth, some scant medical information, a brief report about both the day she was found and her subsequent life at the orphanage. *She is gentle. She likes listening to music. If another child snatches her toy, she will look at the child but not cry, and pick another toy up. If you cuddle her, she will touch your face by her little hands.* The report also said that she weighed about six pounds when she was first found on the streets of Huazhou, on the steps of a pharmacy, lying in a paper box. *She was wearing a suit of gray dress, and covered with a hand-me-down cotton padded coat.*

In her picture she was now twelve months old and she had a beautiful, dainty, heart-shaped face with fine features and an air of serenity. She looked to me like a little, exotic flower. The exotic part was due to her hair, which was dancing all over the place, confident and springy. My pediatrician got upset when I told her about Sasha's head circumference, which the report said was only sixteen inches, and her body weight, which was only sixteen pounds, and her height, which was only twenty-six inches. The doctor, an international adoption specialist, was so upset she had me call our adoption agency and ask them to contact the orphanage and verify. When the stats were confirmed, the doctor had me ask for more photos. She said one way you could tell if a baby had fetal alcohol syndrome was by the vertical lines connecting the nose to the mouth. No lines was a bad sign; defined lines was a good sign. When I got the new pictures I blew them up gigantic on my computer and I studied and studied them for shadows that might reveal lines, but the photo resolution was so bad it was hard to tell what was what. Then something happened, sort of like when you can't find your car and you suddenly realize you're in the whole wrong parking lot, and I made the picture small again and she turned back into a beautiful flower.

The Yahoo! group was wonderful because I got to look at pictures of other babies adopted from Huazhou that people had posted and also I got to hear how everyone loved Miss Peng, the orphanage director, whom many had met and thought to be an angel.

We got the picture in March, right after Anna turned three, and then we had to wait until June to travel to China to go get Sasha. It was hard to know how to fill that big black hole of time. If you didn't fill it with something in particular, it would so easily get plugged with fear and all the tricks of the imagination.

Right away I tried to figure out what her Chinese name meant. Ji Hong Bin. At first I got: Lucky Red Kneecap. Then I got: Lucky Roasted Hair on Temples. Hmm. Translating Chinese into English is something of a fine art. Ji Hong Bin was the "pinyin" version of her name. Pinyin is a system devised to represent Chinese characters phonetically using our alphabet. You have to first get the pinyin translation and then match that to the actual Chinese character. These are not subtle differences. In pinyin "Ji" can mean anything from "lucky" to "horseback" to "accumulate" to "bamboo box used to carry books." And "Hong" will lead you to "red" just as easily as it will to "cistern," "blast," and "species of wild swan."

I was able to get a good match on Ji and Hong. Lucky and

Red. Bin was giving me a lot of trouble. Lucky Red Riverbank? Lucky Red High-Quality Iron? Eventually, I found it. A character with every last squiggle accounted for.

So here was my daughter: Lucky Red Equally-Fine-in-External-Accomplishments-and-Internal-Qualities.

It seemed a big name for such a little girl. But I liked the meaning. The notion of balance. The notion of luck. What a wonderful wish to place upon a six-pound baby lying in a paper box.

One of the things we did while filling up time before going to China was we got goats. I wanted goats because I had heard that they would eat our multiflora rose, the thorny bush that is almost impossible to control, and also because goats are funny. Gretta recommended Nubians, the kind with the long, floppy ears, because they're big and eat a lot and we had so much we needed eaten. I rode with her in her truck to the farm in Ohio and met the girl who raised them and her proud parents and then a month later I learned that the girl's father died suddenly of a heart attack. I sent a card and identified myself as "the lady who bought your goats." It's hard to know the right thing to do in a situation like that.

We named the goats Nellie, Tut, and Cleopatra. Nellie was the oldest and her big ears flew up like Sister Bertrille's hat on *The Flying Nun* whenever she heard any sounds that concerned her. Tut was Nellie's son, and Cleopatra was her pregnant daughter.

Gretta gave us instructions on goat prenatal care. She said

the most important thing was exercise and she suggested we walk Cleopatra twice daily. I never knew you could walk a goat. It was like walking a very obedient dog. Cleopatra never pulled at the leash, or whimpered, or complained about the snow. She and I wandered around the farm, and I talked to her about motherhood because she was just getting started and I was by now getting sure of myself.

We bought an intercom system from Radio Shack so that we could eavesdrop on the actions of our goats in the barn. One night I was giving Anna a bath and we heard horrible goat hollering coming out of the monitor. Alex ran down to the barn. "It's time!" he yelled. Cleopatra, he reported, was in labor. I asked him how he could be so certain. He said there was a foot sticking out.

I pulled Anna out of the tub and quickly dried her hair and bundled her and by the time I ran through the night and into the barn, baby Greg was born; Cleopatra had done all the work. Instinctively, she took on the business of cleaning and nursing—within minutes this goat was a pro. "Congratulations!" I said to her, and closed the barn door to give mother and child a chance to sleep. I thought that was the end of it, and went to bed wondering if there was any sort of message in all of this.

Three days later, George came barreling up our driveway. This was way before we went into our neighbor-feud. This was back when George was just an everyday part of our lives. "I've got something here," he said, climbing out of his pickup. He was carrying a baby lamb. The tiniest creature, about the size of a kitten. Her nose was pink and her body was covered in tight fuzz. George said she was just born a few hours previously. She was one of triplets. Her mother had rejected her, had refused to let her suckle, had kicked her away. He said sheep just do this sometimes. "Maybe you can help?" he said, holding out the orphaned lamb.

I took her in my arms. She was all skin and bones, a wrinkled angel. I asked George how a person went about rescuing a creature so delicate.

"I was more thinking your goat could do it," he said, looking over at Cleopatra. Goats and sheep are genetically similar, he said, and a willing goat can raise a lamb. This was news to me. George said our goat would have more than enough milk for this baby, too. Maybe she would accept her as one of her own. Maybe she wouldn't. It was worth the try. It was either that or let the lamb die.

I felt awkward. How do you go about asking a goat to mother a lamb? I placed the lamb next to where baby Greg was nursing. Cleopatra looked, sniffed, looked some more. In an instant she had made up her mind. The lamb took a good long drink and the bond was formed.

In a way, it was the most natural thing in the world. Here was a creature that needed a mom, and here was a mom with plenty of mothering to give.

I stood there a long time watching this, filled with pride for my goat and her good deed. At one point Cleopatra looked over at me. It wasn't an expression of thanks or even a knowing. It was a plain old goat look of "What are you looking at?" A bond is a bond is a bond.

I remember thinking that if Anna and Sasha ever complain about having gotten me as a mom, I could send them out to talk to that lamb. "Yeah, you think you've got it rough," that lamb could say. "My mom is a goat."

We named her Sweet Pea. Within weeks, well before the daffodils came up, she was strong enough to play in the barnyard, tumbling with Greg and accepting Anna's invitation to wear a hat.

A lot of Americans adopting from China incorporate some portion of their child's Chinese name into the new American name, but with Sasha we couldn't figure out a way to do this, just as we couldn't with Anna. Anna's Chinese name is Gu Yu Qian. We tried Anna Gu Levy or Anna Gu Yu Levy and everything sounded ridiculous and apologetic. "Levy" is so Jewish: you throw Chinese into it and the whole thing sounds too eager to please. So with both girls we decided they'd head into life with two names; they'd have their American names and they'd grow up knowing their Chinese names, too. Gu Yu Qian translates to "Pretty Like Jade." When we went to China to get Anna, I bought a jade bead and a small gold chain and I made a necklace that I never take off. I tried to think of something I could wear around my neck that would say: Lucky Red Equally-Fine-in-External-Accomplishments-and-Internal-Qualities.

Every day I checked the Yahoo! group for help with this and other matters, including tips on how to make rice congee and which stores in Guangzhou had the best deals on baby clothes. Sometimes people would post newspaper articles of interest, and one day this one landed in my in-box:

The Guardian—Final Edition

SECTION: *Guardian Features Pages, pg. 7*

LENGTH: *772 words*

HEADLINE: *Women: Do the foreigners who adopt our girls know how to feed and love them in their arms and hearts?*

BYLINE: *Xinran*

BODY:

Recently I received an e-mail. Had I ever interviewed any women who were forced to give up children because of the "one child" law, which China started in 1981? Yes, many.

One particularly painful memory stands out. On a cold winter morning in 1990, I passed a public toilet in Zhangzhou. A noisy crowd had formed around a little bag of clothes lying in the windy entrance. People were pointing and shouting: "Look, look, she is still alive!"

"Alive? Was this another abandoned baby girl?" I pushed through the crowd and picked up that little bundle: it was a baby girl, barely a few days old. She was frozen blue, but her tiny nose was twitching. I begged for help: "We should save her, she is alive!"

"Stupid woman, do you know what you are doing? How could you manage this poor thing?"

I couldn't wait for help. I took the baby to the nearest hospital.

I paid for first aid for her, but no one in the hospital seemed to be in a hurry to save this dying baby. I took a tape recorder from my backpack and started reporting what I saw. It worked: a doctor stopped and took the baby to the emergency room.

As I waited outside, a nurse said: "Please forgive our cold minds. There are too many abandoned baby girls for us to handle. We have helped more than ten, but afterwards, no one has wanted to take responsibility for their future."

I broadcast this girl's story on my radio show that night. The phone lines were filled with both angry and sympathetic callers.

Ten days later, I got a letter from a childless couple; they wanted to adopt the baby girl. That same day on my answer machine, I heard a crying voice: "Xinran, I am the mother of the baby girl. She was born just four days before you saved her. Thank you so much for taking my daughter to hospital. I watched in the crowd with my heart broken. I followed you and sat outside your radio station all day. Many, many times I almost shouted out to you: 'That is my baby!'

"I know many people hate me; I hate myself even more. But you don't know how hard life is for a girl in the countryside as the first child of a poor family. When I saw their little bodies bullied by hard work and cruel men, I promised I wouldn't let my girl have such a hopeless life. Her father is a good man, but we can't go against our family and the village. We have to have a boy for the family tree.

"Oh, my money is running out, only two minutes left, it is so expensive.

"We can't read or write. But, if you can, please tell my girl in the future to remember that, no matter how her life turns out,

my love will live in her blood and my voice in her heart. (I could hear her crying at this point.) Please beg her new family to love her as if she were their own. I will pray for them every day and . . ."

The message stopped. Three months later, I sent the baby girl to her new family—a schoolteacher and a lawyer—with her new name, "Better." Better's mother never called again.

Afterwards, I started to search for other mothers who had abandoned their girls. This spring, I talked to some near the banks of the Yangtze River. Did they not want to find out where their babies were? "I would rather suffer this dark hole inside me if it means she can have a better life. I don't want to disturb my girl's life," said one. "I am very pleased for a rich person to take my daughter; she has a right to live a good life," said another.

One of them asked me: "Do you believe those foreigners who adopt our girls know how to feed and love them in their arms and hearts?"

I read this article over and over again. The first few times I felt like a spy finally finding the corner of the edge of the most critical piece of evidence that would mean the difference between war and peace. Actual words from the actual ghost-mothers. It is so hard for me to believe these women exist, so hard to hold on to the small fictions I invent to remember the truth that happened before my arrival in my girls' lives. It is as meaningful as imagining the landscape of heaven; I may as well be a kid picturing God up there mixing the potions He'll pour into the molds to now populate Cleveland.

I can't hold on to the fact that my daughters were once cradled by the women who gave them their biology, were once jostled about by aunts or grandmothers who took hold of their umbilical cords and made the cut, were once wiped clean of the goo with which they arrived into the world by some trusted villager. I can't hold on to the fact of her goodbye. I can't hold on to that one at all.

In my mind I begin both of my daughters' lives with the pictures that arrived in the mail. The beautiful babies waiting. To think about the rest of it is only to realize how little I think about the rest of it, is only to spiral down again and down again.

What do I want? What does she want? We want to meet one day, as old women, alone in a coffee shop. We want to embrace and fall into sobs. We want to verify in each other the fulfillment of every mother's pledge: we did the best with what we had. We want to discover an instant kind of love that exceeds all expectations.

Anna came with us to China to get Sasha. To keep her entertained on the plane, I supplied her with many books of stickers. When we arrived in Beijing she had little Poohs and Piglets covering her arms and legs and many people remarked that she looked like one of those tattooed ladies in the circus. Anna remained largely oblivious to the attention and soon enough added Eeyore to the tip of her nose.

Twelve other families were picking up Huazhou babies and so we formed a large group. I could see some of the other parents-to-be studying Anna, and I got the sense that despite the stickers she became for them a symbol of hope. Here was the healthiest child in the world, a happy kid with a rich imagination who just two years previously had been bundled up in an orphanage, waiting.

It was June and unbearably hot in Beijing but nonetheless we all traveled to the Forbidden City, where we took pictures for our girls to one day hold. Then we went to the Great Wall and bought pearls. Alex and I had both learned when we got Anna that these trips aren't about sightseeing. Your whole self is used up trying to learn how to be a parent and there is nothing left. Even so, there is the rumble of who you used to be, the person who traveled the world in search of stories and who fell in love with wandering way back as a kid on Lorraine Drive, taking off for a day in the woods. The adventure! Standing on the Great Wall stretching east and west into the horizon, it was hard to be just a person with a camera and a seat waiting on a bus. I wanted to run on that wall. I wanted to climb. But Anna was hot and she needed more juice.

Women who have babies early in life often think of motherhood as a rut, as if there's a great world beyond they're somehow missing out on. But I remember wishing for babies as a young woman, feeling my life of adventure was a rut. I try not to make too much of this. Mostly, I just think life is full of ruts. There's the rut of putting the coffee on the exact same way you did the night before, first the water, then the filter, then eight scoops, then the button setting the timer so that at 6 a.m. you'll smell it brewing. The rut of waking up to your same radio station, same announcer, same robe, same slippers, same dogs to let out, vitamins, cat snaking between your legs. The rut of the same bowl of Kix for your kid, same yogurt, same highchair, Elmo. The rut of eating a banana at your desk while checking your e-mail. The rut of: Aren't I getting boring? *Shouldn't I perk this life up?*

Did I want a second kid simply to get out of a rut? Is that why I wanted the first one? Where would this method of family planning end up?

When we got to Guangzhou the next day, it was even hotter than Beijing and the smog was so bad our guides told us to try to stay in the hotel from 10 a.m. to 5 p.m. We boarded a bus to the place where Sasha was said to be waiting for us. We entered an office building and all you heard were babies crying, it sounded like a thousand of them. We waited in a room and Alex held the video camera and his shirt was completely wet with sweat. One by one they brought the babies in and yelled out their names. It was all so hot and chaotic and I wondered where Miss Peng was. A woman was wandering around with a baby in her arms and she was saying, "Ji Hong Bin? Ji Hong Bin?" And at first I shook my head no. Then I heard her say it again and I looked at the baby.

I recognized her eyes. Nothing else. Her hair had been shaved off and she was so tiny she did not look entirely real. Her eyes, just her eyes were huge. They were dark as crude oil and pleading. I held out my arms and when she fell inside it was nothing like it was with Anna. Anna had been a bowl of Jell-O, an armful of peace.

Sasha was a solid jangle of bones, stiff as sticks. I knew she was sick. At that moment I thought: cerebral palsy. Anna reached up to her with a toy but Sasha didn't take it.

I wondered again where Miss Peng was. Everyone had said she was an angel and yet she wasn't even here to deliver this group of children. She had something better to do?

I wondered what these monsters had done to this child.

I looked at Alex as I fell into tears. He turned off the camera and came running and when he took Sasha in his arms she clung to him like a starving monkey. She did not let go.

Ten million people live in Guangzhou and yet it's only China's fifth-largest city. We rode back to the hotel in the bus and I held Anna and smelled her hair and Sasha was still clinging to Alex. I was sick of all those ten million people. I was missing my rut back home. It was all so circular, so Dorothy, so Auntie Em. You could write an ode to your own backyard if so many people hadn't already thought of it.

Our room was on the twenty-second floor of the hotel and Anna loved running down the long hallway. It was exactly as it was the day before, when we checked in, except now Alex had a little monkey stuck to him.

In our room we peeled off Sasha's clothes, a light jumpsuit two sizes too big. She did not mind this or anything else. Her legs were twigs. She seemed profoundly malnourished. She was silent and tight, holding her arms to her chest. We sat her on the floor and surrounded her with toys. She looked but did not reach for any of them, despite Anna's repeated attempts to offer them. "Why won't my sister play with me?" Anna asked. I told her to wait. I told myself to wait. But worry had already swept in and through me and now sat on my chest like a stone. What was wrong with her? What was wrong with my baby?

Was the treatment she received at the orphanage so poor that she was somehow shell-shocked? Had she ever been loved at all? Had she ever been held? Had she ever played with a toy?

I tried to sympathize, to understand the ghost-mother and all the ghost-nannies. But forgiveness was so far away now.

I tried to empathize, to put myself in Sasha's heart. She had just been yanked away from the only family she'd ever known: on the one hand an orphanage, but on the other hand a home. There is a level of comfort in any rut—any.

But Anna hadn't been like this. In her first day with us, Anna was already a playful girl who could play peekaboo and who giggled with abandon.

Sasha sat on that spot on the floor and followed us with eyes that seemed to drink. All my hope was in those eyes. She was in there. There was a person inside that stone child. At one point, and not by design, Alex and Anna and I were all in the bathroom, leaving Sasha alone. We heard a noise. A moan that sounded not quite human. We rushed back into the room and found her there, doubled over, her head bent to her feet.

It was a howl of abandonment we would hear again and again, if even for a moment she was left alone. She was in there. There was a person inside that stone child.

We tried to feed her but she wouldn't eat.

We tickled her but she wouldn't smile.

I didn't sleep at all those first nights. I wanted her to be different. I wanted her to be healthy and happy and easy. I prayed to God and promised I would care for her. It was more will than honor speaking.

The next day I broke down and let everything out, falling into heavy sobs of grief. "What are we going to do?" I said to Alex.

He wasn't sure what I meant. That was interesting. Alex held none of my same worry. I told him what I meant. There was something wrong with our baby. Those monsters had done something to our baby. "What are we going to do?" I said, pleading.

"I think you should start believing in her," he answered.

Those words formed an echo in my head that would come back at me again and again for days until I didn't need them anymore. *I think you should start believing in her.*

We went to the pool. The air was so thick with smog everything was yellow and my contact lenses were so foggy I saw rainbows. A woman from our group was in the pool with her baby. The child seemed, to me, even worse off than Sasha. She was a few months older and just as thin and just as stone-faced and she didn't even have eyes that followed. And yet that woman cooed at her baby and told her how beautiful she was and she went on bragging about her to the rest of us.

I never told her this, but that woman became my model and my champion. I watched her the next day in the pool and I watched her on the bus and in the hotel restaurant and I watched her in the gift shop. I tried her on as you would a costume.

At first it was hard squeezing belief out of air. But the belief enabled me to coo with Sasha and cuddle with her as you would a two-day-old infant. I whispered in her ear about her pretty bald head. "You know, a lot of girls can't get away with a look like this, but you're so pretty you pull it off!" I clapped when she ate a spoonful of rice and I bought her pretty outfits in the gift shop and I tried them on her. Anna and I stuck bows on her head with tape and applauded.

One morning I took her for a walk, just the two of us. We strolled through the small park outside our hotel where a few hundred people would cram each morning to practice tai chi on the bank of the Pearl River. They dressed in loose clothes and sandals and the women hung their handbags off the branches of the sycamore trees. One group brandished swords, another danced with giant red fans, but most just had liquid arms and legs and backs and necks, their moves as fluid as the river carrying too many barges behind them. It seemed an exhausted river, an exhausted city, polluted and crowded and yet somehow finding the energy to keep going on like this, day after day, and I held Sasha and promised to bring her back here someday.

When we got back to the room, Anna was on the bed playing with Cheerios, dumping them into and out of cups. I sat Sasha next to her and she watched with those eyes that held so much. Anna saw her watching and paused. She took a Cheerio and held it out to her sister.

Sasha unfolded one arm, and reached out for the Cheerio. She took it and examined it.

"Look! Look! Look what she did!" Anna said. It was as if Sasha had reached through a thousand centuries. It was a gesture that said, "Yeah, okay, I'm in." Or, "Hello, family, and thanks for waiting." It was her first real act of acknowledgment.

I went to my computer and wrote to everyone back home,

"Sasha took a Cheerio! Sasha took a Cheerio!" wondering how to fully convey the implications. Later that day, Anna put on her purple tutu and ran in circles around the room while Sasha watched. When Anna leapt on the bed with a great flourish, Sasha turned to me as if to make sure I had seen that terrific move. I nodded with a smile. And that was when Sasha did it. It seemed painful, as if these muscles were put to use for the first time, so naturally they were stiff. But there it was. Sasha's first smile.

We got out the camera and tried to get her to do it again. We spent most of our time in China this way, succeeding in fits and starts until pretty soon the smiles came all on their own. Her body relaxed, her arms came away from her chest, and by the time we returned to the farm the person who is Sasha began to emerge.

One morning at the farm I was pouring her a bowl of Kix and the cat was snaking between my legs and Anna was using her pink yogurt as finger paint. I told Sasha, I said, "Welcome to our rut."

She had sprouted two teeth on the bottom and some of her hair was coming in, taking the shine off her bald head.

a cold front

"We're going to lose our light," the small man said to the tall man. They were from the city. The tall man was the apprentice. He had to carry all the equipment, and I remember thinking how strong he was, how he didn't complain, how in so many ways he made a good mule.

They were taking pictures of the area for a magazine and they wanted me to tell them how the sun went. They were standing on my front porch. I said, well, you see how this house sits at the bottom of a bowl? If we climbed the eastern ridge, to the lip of the bowl, we'd be able to watch the sun make its slow crimson descent. We headed up the path. They said what many people from the city say when they get off concrete. They said it's colder here. They said the air is clean. They said it's so quiet.

We heard something by the pond. We heard an animal

crying. But we were in a hurry to catch the sun, so at first we ignored it. The noise got louder. "What is that sound?" the tall man said, finally. The question had to be asked, and once it was asked we had to look. Just off the main path, in a tumble of leaves, we saw an orange kitten, almost big enough to be called a cat, a teenage cat.

"It's stuck in the brambles," I told them, going over to free the cat. It was twisting and turning in the oddest way. It didn't look crazy sick. I didn't fear it exactly. I've met so many cats in these woods.

I picked up the cat. It wasn't stuck on anything. I put it down on the path and said, "Go on, now." The cat tried to go on. The front of it twisted and struggled to free itself from the back of it, which didn't work.

"Looks like maybe the back legs are broken," the small man said.

The small man and the tall man looked at me.

I said, "Well, wait a second, I can't take any more cats."

I wanted to explain to them, but I didn't want to explain to them, how it works. I didn't want to spoil the clean air. People drop off kittens. People can't figure out what to do with them, so they drop them in the woods. The animal shelters can't take any more kittens. My own rescues have produced mixed results. The last time was a year ago, a litter of two. My daughter named one Elmo and the other one Elmo. We put them in the barn for the night. In the morning we came out and found that our poodle had killed Elmo. He does this. He does this with a passion that is half savage and half casual. Fifty-fifty. He just does this. We buried Elmo by the apple tree, and then I took

Elmo up to my office and kept him in there until he became a full-grown cat. It took months of convincing. Finally, the dog seems to understand that Elmo is a part of the family, and not a potential trophy.

I didn't want to explain this. I didn't want to even think what my dog would do to a disabled cat. And, anyway, we were losing our light. In the country you build up calluses. There is so much to save. You can't save everything. The fact becomes a plain, hard shell.

"When you see something like this," the tall man said, looking at the cat, "you have two choices. You put it out of its misery, or you find help." It seemed such an obvious statement and yet courageous all the same. We agreed. We talked about ways of killing it. I said there was no way. The small man shook his head. The tall man said, "Then it's up to me." It seemed we were characters in a parable, something in the Bible or a children's book. You read those things and imagine yourself the good one, the smart one, the hero. Only when you're actually in the story do you find all the reasons for being the one who just stood by. It doesn't excuse you. It doesn't really help at all. The tall man stared and thought and in the end said he'd take the cat away and figure something out. We brought it to his car, put it inside, then raced to the top of the ridge to capture the sun.

That was a Saturday. Weeks went by and I heard nothing. Pretty soon the cat and the tall man and the small man would be just another few characters I once met, characters you hold out hope for while busily denying this and that.

Then one day I got a fax. It was a report from a veterinarian's office. *Spot is four-pound tabby, does not appear to be in pain, legs severely damaged beyond repair. Probably hit by a car at just weeks old. Severely malnourished. Spot may still have a good-quality life. I would try to find her a home before more drastic measures are taken.* The fax was followed by a call from the tall man. He lived in a one-bedroom apartment and often had trouble just making the rent. "I hate to ask you this, but any amount would help . . ." I said, of course! He said Spot could get around fine now, dragging her back legs behind her. He said he never wanted a cat. He said looking at that cat was like looking at happiness.

speechless

We took a family vacation to Aruba because John Daller, our accountant, has a time share there and one year he couldn't use it. We saw the poster when we were in his office getting our taxes done and I happened to mention motherhood's attendant exhaustion and the fact that I was having prison fantasies. "I was thinking how it really wouldn't be so bad, just for a little while." I'd actually caught myself having a daydream of a most pleasant afternoon in a place where there's nothing to do but sit and stare at a cinderblock wall.

Ask any mother just what, exactly, is so exhausting about motherhood and she will likely have a hard time pinpointing it. The problem is, you block it out. The minute you get a break from motherhood, all those details of what, exactly, was wearing you out are . . . gone. Poof! Disappeared. This is an evolutionary phenomenon, a way the species protects itself. Any mother who can't get rid of the memories of how exhausting mothering is would have to kill herself, leaving all those half-grown kids to fend for themselves.

One thing I know is that it's really not just the lack of sleep. It's really not just the fact that Sasha wakes up several times a night because she kicked her blanket off and somehow I'm the only one with the skills to get it back on right—must-be-Mommy—oh, Daddy's blanket-covering prowess is just not up to snuff according to the little snit of a kid who has you awake *again,* and there you stand knowing you'll *never* get back to sleep now because now you just remembered that Anna grew out of her sneakers and so what the heck is she going to wear on her feet when she goes on the pony ride at the birthday party that you can't believe you have to go to, and hang on, did you buy wrapping paper? No, you most certainly did not. So, think, *think!* Well, you can have the girls make homemade wrapping paper out of old grocery bags and markers and stickers and make it look like you planned it, oh my God, it will be so cute, and speaking of cute, what is the *matter* with you that you are not the kind of mother who sews, you have yet to make your kids one outfit and you never even tried to crochet either of them an afghan. Dud! *Dud!* Shame on you! You're a dud of a mother. . . .

No, the no-sleep issue is not the meat of the problem, I don't think. Exhaustion as it pertains to motherhood is more specifically related to the fact that it's so damn constant. As mother, you are the sergeant of an army and most of the time your soldiers don't do what you tell them to, and not only that but they fight, pick at each other, a flick of a pea, a stolen potato chip, and then they want more juice, even though you said no more juice they want more juice, so you offer milk because their teeth are going to fall out from all that juice, and then they cry and the negotiations continue and you dig your heels in because *your job is to build character,* and the only way to build character is to set boundaries, and enforce them. Then one of them has to go potty, and the other one has you looking under the sofa for a lost teapot that goes with the little mouse tea party set you knew had too many parts, and so you put your hand under the couch and you find a half-eaten Pop-Tart, which enrages you far more than it should. And so you yell and they cry and you would cry, too, if you stopped to think about how the only hope you have for sanity is a Barney video. You put the Barney video in and they ask for more juice.

Anybody can survive a day of this, of course; anyone can survive a week. But the thing about child rearing is, those children who grow up so fast don't really, not when you break it down hour-by-hour and minute-by-minute. They don't stop being children, not even for a day, not even for a weekend, while they are busily growing up so fast, and sooner or later you ask yourself: How is it that I've turned into such a cranky foam-at-the-mouth bitch when I was always the fun one, the fun aunt, the lady who would visit my nieces and nephews and be welcomed like a reprieve from the monster my sister somehow turned into? "You're funny! I wish *you* were my mom!" That's what they said and so you always thought, *Wow, I'm going to be a great mom.* And now here you are an actual mom with your very own kids and they are finding someone else to say it to—"You're funny! I wish *you* were my mom!"—maybe a babysitter, or one of your good friends from college; the thing of it is, you don't even *care*. Whatever, so your kids think you're a horrible grouch of a mom and they'd rather have a fun mom, uh-huh, whatever, can we just wrap this up and get on with the business of baths?

Maybe one of the reasons I even had the prison fantasy was because of the notion of already having been convicted. Whew. Done. Now let me get myself into my cell, and, by the way, is there any chance I could upgrade to a padded one?

And so. There we were sitting in our accountant's office, and John Daller our accountant pointed to the poster of the time share in Aruba, a glorious photo of an azure blue sea with a little coconut-tree hut in the foreground. And that was that.

When we got to Aruba, I sat in one of those very same huts and I wore a big hat and I tried to read a book. That used to be a very enjoyable activity but now it was a war of conscience. The problem is, a lot can happen to a four-and-a-half-year-old child while you are sneaking your way into a chapter, and even more can happen to a two-and-a-half-year-old. Every little paragraph felt like a naughty treat and then I would imagine explaining to the ambulance driver that I just *had* to turn the page to find out if the wife really was cheating or not—it was coming up on the next page!—and that's all I did, I just read that one tiny next paragraph and then when I looked up my kid was hanging from the jaws of that shark; *I swear I had no idea how she even got into the water in the first place!*

It's not worth it, all the places your imagination takes you when you are stealing your way out of motherhood and into being a normal person who just wants to read a damn book on the beach.

My friend Nancy told me that going on vacation wasn't the same once you were a mom, but I think she held back telling me the whole thing. Her husband, Jack, is a good father, and so is my husband. These are not the type of men to go off to the casino or even to put back bourbons. They are "family" men who want nothing more than to be right there in family mode, sticking always by our sides. Even so, it always comes back to the mother to keep the kids from getting bitten by crabs or scorched by the sun or electrocuted by putting their fingers in the sockets of the little speakers put around so the vacationers can enjoy calypso music.

In Aruba, Sasha wore a pink bikini with pictures of turtles on it. She wasn't talking yet but I wasn't worried. When people asked me how old she was, I said two, leaving out the "and a half" part, and I think that little slip, that omission, was probably a good indicator of the denial I was in. Kids at two and a half are supposed to have a vocabulary of about three hundred words. Sasha had seven, but only if you really stretched it. She had three reliable sounds: "Ma," meaning "Mom," "Dat," meaning "Dad," and "Iss," meaning "this," and which she would use while pointing to get whatever she needed. "Iss" was a refined version of her former "sss" sound she would use as her one and only all-purpose word.

No, I told myself, I really wasn't worried. After all, Anna had been very slow to talk, too. Anna said nothing but "ch" for an entire year. I was used to this, to Lisa, the speech therapist who would come to our house with her Pooh toys two times a week and clap as Anna learned new sounds. Plenty of kids who come out of orphanages from China don't have speech delays at all, but plenty do. Lisa had seen her share. Her theory was simple and shared by many of those experts who write in language-acquisition journals: disruption at about a year old is at a critical stage in language development—the very time the child is starting to mimic the people in the world around her. So, imagine, one day it's all music and tone and *ee-ow,* and then, bam, the next it's a strange nasal mess of clicks and clacks. The development shuts down, while the pathways in the brain rejigger themselves. But soon enough, with patience and some speech therapy to boost and encourage, language emerges again, and anew.

By the time Anna was three she was well on her way to speaking, although her path to language was the weirdest Lisa and her colleagues had ever observed. Rather than imitating sounds, the key for Anna was the alphabet. The actual symbols. She loved those things. We'd be at the grocery store and see a sign for grapes and Anna would run up and point. "G!" she'd say, looking at the sign and giving me a look of "Can you believe it? G is here!"

The symbols were her friends. When Lisa couldn't get her to say "ball," she finally picked up a block with a "B" on it. "Buh buh buh," she said, pointing to the letter. That got Anna's attention. ("Yay! B is here!") And so she would mimic "buh" and that got her revved up to go all the way into "ball." And so came word after word.

I was eager for Anna to speak because I felt she would have so much to say. I felt I would get to know her better when she finally had a spoken form for her thoughts. What, anyway, is a person without language? Who is a girl with nothing more to offer than "ch" or "sss"?

When Anna finally started talking, the thing I learned was how much she loved the alphabet, the actual symbols, and she also loved numbers, the actual symbols, she loved them in blue and in pink and in red and in combinations aplenty.

The thing is, she was the same girl she was when all she said was "ch." She was just . . . a little more so. She was growing up and into herself. I'm not convinced words changed anything, even though the thought disappoints me. I wanted language to be the key, not for Anna so much as my exalted sense of language. I spend my days with words, putting my thoughts into written form. Giving language to my thoughts is the only way I even know what my thoughts are. Anyone knows that words are what separate us from the rest of the animal kingdom. Surely language is where people *begin* being people.

This, anyway, is the indoctrination. This is the assumption you walk around with, having been schooled on the principle of words as the building blocks of communication. True enough. But what about the stuff underneath the building blocks? The rocks and the dirt and the mud of emotion? Like all babies, Anna laughed long before she spoke; she laughed in my arms the first day I held her. Jokes are funny in Chinese and in Arabic and in French and in Infant-ese. A bassoon can tell a joke and so can a flute and a cat can do something very, very funny. But among creatures, only people can laugh. Laughter, I think, is where people begin being people.

I wanted Sasha to have a breakthrough just as Anna had had with the alphabet. Lisa started coming to our house in May of that year, when Sasha was twenty-six months old, and she tested Sasha every which way. Sasha proved to be on target for cognitive development as well as fine-motor development, while ahead of the game, testing at the level of a twenty-nine-month-old, for gross-motor skills. *Today Sasha was observed to throw a ball at least three feet and walked along a line of tape on the floor. Sasha can do a somersault with ease.*

Language acquisition in children is divided into two components: receptive, meaning the words the child comprehends, and expressive, the words she can actually say. Sasha scored on target for receptive. *She is beginning to respond to basic prepositions such as "in," "out," "on." Sasha also can identify several body parts and will point to pictures in a book when asked.* But her expressive-language development was placed at a paltry fourteen months. She was a toddler with the communication skills of an infant.

There was one line in Lisa's report that none of us made a big enough deal of at the time: *Sasha tends to point and use gestures creatively to express her wants/needs.*

Creatively.

In Aruba there was a playground on the beach near the little coconut-tree hut and my girls were playing and so were two older girls, maybe eight and ten, both with long blonde hair. Anna was busy smushing wet sand through her toes and fingers and then painting her legs with "A," "B," and "C" and then making designs on her cheeks like war paint. Anna has always been this way. She can entertain herself with a stone and a feather.

Sasha was watching the blonde-haired girls. At first I thought it was their acrobatics that caught her attention. The older girls had mastered the swinging bridge made of hanging tires and soon enough they took to leaping off it and then diving into somersaults in the sand. Sasha watched and watched with those eyes that held so much, those eyes that held so much in China when she was in my arms for the first time, a frozen little girl with a bald head and arms curled into her chest in fear. And now here she was a nineteen-pound peanut in a pink bikini.

In one swift motion, Sasha picked up a shell and walked over to the smaller of the two girls. She offered the shell to the girl. "Oh, thank you," the girl said, taking it. And so Sasha picked up another shell and offered it to the other girl, who likewise took it.

"Aw, she's so cute!" said one to the other.

Sasha did not smile. Instead, she held out her hands and demanded both shells back.

The girls obliged, giggling.

All three stood there for a moment.

"Iss!" Sasha said, looking at the shells. Then she dropped them, one in front of each girl. She pointed to the ground. "Iss!"

"She-is-so-cute!" the taller girl said to the other, both

seeming to instinctively understand the order to bend down and pick up the shells. And so they obeyed.

I felt as if I was watching some sort of mating dance, with Sasha in charge. All action, no language. And yet she was so willing and so able to communicate an invitation for friendship—a friendship on her terms.

In time the girls were at the bottom of the sliding board, encouraging Sasha, who was at the top of it. "Come on! You can do it! We'll catch you!"

Sasha sat up there and pondered. Then she waved her hand in a wiping motion. "Iss!" she shouted.

"You want us to wipe off the slide?" the short one asked her. Sasha nodded in the affirmative.

"There's *sand* on the slide!" the tall one said. "We have to get it *off*!"

So they did, while the little peanut in the pink turtle bikini sat on high and watched and waited. A queen. A ruler. A girl for whom language was a royal waste of time.

Eventually, the girls approached me. They told me they were cousins, Julia and Jennifer. "Will you be here tomorrow?" asked Julia. "Because we would like to play with her after Bingo."

I told them we would be and they jumped with happiness. "High five?" Jennifer said to Sasha, holding up her hand for a slap. Sasha had no clue what this meant and so the girls taught her.

After that, we spent every afternoon in Aruba with Jennifer and Julia, both of them waiting on Sasha and occasionally waiting on Anna but just to be polite. The thing that got me was the realization that Sasha would spend her life being pop-

ular, demanding it, getting it. I figured Anna would or wouldn't
be, but probably wouldn't care.

It was easy to see that Sasha's claim on the world predated
her mastery of spoken words. I wondered how much of that was
true of all of us. Before we learn to say hello, have we learned
how to be, how to manage who we are? I always thought language was the key to knowing, to understanding, and maybe
that's true except when it comes to knowing the self. We all cry
and we all laugh before we speak. We are emotion first, thought
second. And I suppose word whenever we get around to it.

That summer Sasha said her first sentence. "Beez a beez a beez
a beez?" This means, "May I please be excused?" We all knew it
the minute she said it, thanks to her posture and beckoning
with her eyes, but mostly because Anna confirmed it. Further
complicating Sasha's attempt to talk was the fact that Anna
understood much of what she said. When you have an interpreter, you aren't as motivated to learn the local lingo.

There was still a lot of summer left so I decided to have the
girls help me cut a path through the woods. Together we would
snip, snip, snip through the sticker bushes and make it to the
top of the hill.

"Be careful of those jaggers," Anna said to Sasha.

"Jaggers" was a word she must have picked up in preschool.
It's a Western Pennsylvania word. I was born in Eastern Pennsylvania, where we said "sticker bushes."

"Anna," I said. "We don't say 'jaggers'; we say 'sticker
bushes.' "

" 'Sticker bushes'?"

"Yeah."

"Sasha," she said. "Be careful of the sticker bushes because they can hurt your fingies." She paused. "Mom, do we say 'fingies'?"

"Sure."

This was how we talked. This was who we were. We never said "butt." We said "bummy." We always said please and thank you and before we left the table we all said, "Beez a beez a beez a beez?" ever since Sasha invented it.

Every family has a language and this was ours. You bring jaggers or sticker bushes from your youth, and then there were all those invented words like "fingies" and "eggy-egg" and "niptydoops" that mysteriously fly in, if only for a little while, like colorful birds.

"Momma," Anna said. "Does Daddy say 'sticker bushes'?"

"Yes, he does," I said. (Or he would now.)

We were about three feet into the impossible thicket. I could see a small clearing on the other side of a partition of thorns, a break. A destination. We were working single file. I snipped, they stomped. We had never embarked on a project nearly this ambitious. I figured it would take months, a little each week. There was no rush. We didn't need the path. There were plenty of other avenues up the hill. I loved the woods and wanted a reason to introduce the girls to them.

I began to think of the woods in the same way I thought of Sasha's language. A new path. A clearing. A deliberate attempt to get from here to there.

"What about this one?" Anna asked, pointing to an innocuous branch on the ground.

"Well, that's the kind you just step over," I said. "We don't have to cut that one."

"We're not going to cut this one?" she said, disappointed.

"Honey, you can just step over stuff. We don't have to cut every single thing."

"Come on, Sash," she said. "We have to step over this one."

I imagined, one day, when the girls are ten and twelve or sixteen and eighteen, walking with them on this path, reminiscing about this time. I imagined a time when they're thirty-four and thirty-six and I'm hobbled with arthritic knees, watching squirrels collecting acorns from the corner of my nursing home window. They'll be out here together, just for old times, saying, "Can you believe Mom made us do this?"

"Sasha, say 'sticker bush,'" Anna said. "Sticker bush? Stiiiiicker buuuuush?"

"Ssss," Sasha said.

"No, that's not right, Sash."

"Ssss," Sasha said more urgently. I looked to see she was pointing at a stick on the ground.

"That's right, sweetie, we're not going to cut that one. That's the kind you just step over."

"Sss! Sss!" Sasha said, her frustration growing.

"Anna, what is she saying?"

"I don't know, Mommy. I don't know!"

"Sss!" Sasha implored. "Sss!" Her face got red. She began blinking furiously. "Sss!"

And then she started to cry.

"What is she saying? What? What is the matter?"

"I don't know, Mommy! I don't know!" Anna kept saying. "SSS!"

Anna started to cry.

It went on like this, two children crying over nothing, or maybe one crying over something and the other over nothing, the one feeding the other.

"Okay, okay, it's okay!" I said.

I picked up Sasha and I held Anna's hand. We headed home and I never found out what happened.

One day I was in the shower shampooing and I heard a horrible sound that might have been a tree falling on our house. But it was quicker than that. It wasn't a boom or a thump or a pow, but a crack, sharp and angry. Then: nothing.

I came charging out of the shower, ran down to the kitchen, where Alex and the girls were eating eggs. All three were mid-chew, their eyes bugged out. "What was that?" "Are you okay?" "What was that?" Something big had happened. Outside, the rain was beating on the geraniums.

"My, what a big noise!" I said cheerfully, but the girls picked up my fear and reached for comfort. Together we tiptoed around the house, looking for the answer to the noise. In the living room we smelled smoke. We saw a hole in the wall, about the size of a quarter, with scorch marks around the edges. "Okay, we were hit by lightning," Alex said. Overreacting, but maybe not, I took the girls outside and we sat in the car above the safety of rubber tires while Alex investigated, making sure our home wasn't about to blow up. After a few minutes he seemed pretty sure it wasn't.

So many things were . . . off. A clock had fallen off the wall. There were holes in the gutters. There were more holes in the living room walls. A jar of peanut butter had jumped off the dining room table and landed upside down on a chair. It seemed the work of ghosts. Skippy, our mule, was out there chasing one of our four fat geese. The goose, white and flapping, appeared terrified. Skippy had never shown any interest in the geese before. "Skippy, leave that goose alone!" There had been a pot of petunias on the picnic table near where the goose was flapping—but the pot was missing. The petunias were right where they had been before the storm, centered on the picnic table, but the pot was four feet away on the ground. How did the pot get out from under the petunias?

It seemed like a whole bunch of magic tricks were going on with no real purpose or scheme; the lightning had just done a random reformatting of things. Nothing seemed too crazy and so at one point I went and checked on Sasha to see if the lightning had given her the gift of speech.

"Iss," she said, pointing to the TV, which was also now broken.

I wondered if this was a sin of some sort, wishing a lightning-inspired miracle upon my child. I wondered if that was tantamount to suggesting to God that I thought my child *needed* a miracle, that His work up to that point wasn't quite up to snuff.

I went to find Alex to get his opinion on the matter, but he was busy in the bathroom noticing that the ceiling fan was blown. It once was white but now it was brown, burnt around the edges. The lightning had zapped it, too.

"You were standing under this thing, soaking wet," Alex correctly pointed out. I was right here in the shower when the lightning came into our house and mixed everything up and burnt holes in our walls. "I just don't understand why it didn't zap through you, too," he said.

We stood there staring up at the burnt ceiling fan.

"Jeeezus—" he said.

I walked around with that one for the rest of the summer and into the fall, noticing a most fervent and eager desire to stay alive. Poof! It could have been me, fried from the inside out with one quick zap. Poof! I imagined over and over again and too many times what would happen to Alex and to the girls if I up and died; I imagined all the trouble, all the subtracting, and then I went to get all the routine checkups I was overdue on. My gynecologist told me I had fibrocystic breasts—she said they were like oatmeal—not that that in itself was a problem, just that I'd need a diagnostic mammogram, not a regular one, meaning they would take extra pictures and maybe do a sonogram. The mammogram place was all atriums and skylights, very modern and cheerful, and try as she might the radiologist with the long ponytail just couldn't get the look she wanted. She kept calling me back in for more X-rays, and more, and more, and in between X-rays I sat in that dark room with the sound of little fans whirring and waited. "We're just going to have to take another." This went on for more than two hours with no one explaining anything to me, which I did not take as a good sign. Waiting in a room alone like that, waiting for someone to come tell you what sort of monstrous tumor they were all so fascinated by, or ten monstrous tumors, or perhaps sixteen smaller ones, waiting in the dark like that is a fine time to take note of exactly just how far fear can propel the imagination. Soon I found myself curled up into a tight little ball, arms wrapped around my legs and feet purple and freezing, and I was in tears. The crying wasn't about dying so much, not about fear of the great unknown—really any of that. The crying was buried in the thought: Well, now what? Another mother gone. First the ghost-mother, then the adoptive mother; they'd see pictures of me in their scrapbook. *Remember her? Oh, yeah, she's one of those moms we had early on, right?* Another mother gone. How much subtraction could these girls take?

Nothing, as it turned out, was wrong with me. They didn't find any tumors or even pre-tumors. And I didn't get hit by lightning. And my blood pressure was normal and so was my cholesterol. Nothing was wrong with me except that now, in a way I never knew before, now I was a person who couldn't read a book on the beach, now I was a person who knew a kind of tired that went deep into my bones, the fatigue of mothering that could lead a person into prison fantasies. Now, really for the first time, now I mattered.

fashion statement

We're working in the barn, putting down some hay. Anna in this moment is just two and a half. She has hold of a rake, and she's mirroring my every move. Except I do not have a pink tutu around my waist to negotiate. The tutu, which features several layers of tulle, each edged with sparkles, has an elastic waist. Thank goodness. How else would it fit over her snow jacket? It's an amusing look, the sort that would send a lot of parents running for cameras, and later, into slaps of laughter. *Oh, look at that silly getup you put on that day!*

I have stacks of pictures like this. I stopped taking tutu pictures months ago, when it became clear that this was more than just a moment to capture. Anna now wears her tutu to the playground, to the grocery store, to the zoo, to bed, everywhere. I keep two backup tutus hidden in a drawer in case of emergency. Like so many little girls her age, she has embraced dance. She's a twirler, a slider, a leaper. Recently she learned that, somewhere in this world, there are tap shoes. She saw a girl in a movie going *clickety clack* with her feet, and understood it as destiny.

"Oh, I'll die if my kid goes into a tutu stage," my friend Wendy said. "But don't feel too embarrassed. She's bound to grow out of it." Embarrassed? It had actually never occurred to me to be embarrassed, although I was certainly getting weary of the questions from strangers. (No, Anna is not now enrolled in ballet lessons. Yes, she probably will be someday. Uh-huh, she sure loves that tutu.) But embarrassed? I wasn't, after all, the one in the tutu. Nor was I, however, ignorant of the reality that a child's outfit can be a billboard announcing the parenting style of the attached parent. *Hello, world, I am a mother who allows her kid to pick out her own clothes. Yup.* I figured the tutu stage might be a dry run for a day about eleven years from now when Anna comes home with green hair and lots of nose piercings. How will I be? Will I be a parent who encourages self-expression? Or one who cracks the whip and disciplines free-thinking right out? I believe, at least in the abstract, in the lessons taught by the former. "I am a parent who encourages self-expression!" I announced to Wendy, and I fluffed Anna's tutu. This was back before she wore out her white tutu, precipitating a need for a purple, which she wore out; we have recently moved on to pink.

"Oh man, if it were me I'd toss the tutus," my sister Claire said. She has three kids, two of them toddlers, and said the tutu deal would not fly in her house. *"Mom is in charge in our house."*

First Wendy, now Claire. Busted. Apparently, I was indulging my child by allowing her to have as much tutu as she wanted. Like sugar. I got defensive. I said lots of kids have security blankets, binkies they haven't grown out of, stuffed animals with little stuffing left. Surely good parenting isn't a matter of depriving your child of the thing that makes her feel secure.

"No," Claire said. "But you need to set limits to establish who's boss." Of course. I reevaluated my stance on the tutu issue, which really hadn't been an issue before. *Be the boss. Establish boundaries. Set rules as to when the tutu is acceptable and when it is not.*

Yes, well. I suppose I haven't made a lot of progress. Exhibit A: the tutu over the snow jacket that Anna is sporting today. When is this going to end? What have I done? Is it too late?

"Okay, sweetie, I think we're done here," I say, wrapping up the twine from the distributed bales of hay. "Let's go up to the house and get cleaned up." We have errands to run, a day of shopping. Anna does not want to get changed. Anna wants to wear this same outfit to the mall. As if. Does she think I'm some pushover of a mother? "Listen, we do not wear stinky barn clothes to the mall," I say, all strict and righteous. "That is the *rule.*"

Soon enough she agrees to clean purple slacks and a clean purple shirt, and when it comes time to choose coats, she picks her favorite leopard-print faux fur. "Anna's tutu?" she says, handing it to me.

"Are you sure, honey?" I say.

She throws me a look that is half horror and half exasperation. *You expect me to go out in public without a tutu?*

I take a deep breath. I help her get the tutu on. The coat is thick and robs her of any semblance of a waist, so the tutu is about as wide up top as it is at the bottom. "Glasses?" she says. "Anna's glasses?" She finds her sunglasses, a purple plastic pair given to her by her otherwise wise and loving father.

Well, then. She looks up at me. *Are you ready?*

At the mall, I don't bother looking at the people staring. I don't want to talk about it. Yeah, this is my fabulous child. Yeah, I'm the mother of the girl in the getup. I try to get Wendy's voice out of my head, and Claire's. I am a mother who encourages self-expression. Surely there is something good about this.

The display in the front of the Payless shoe store calls Anna as if put there by her own private angel. "Tap shoes!" she cries. "Tap shoes!" An entire rack of shiny patent leather shoes with bright silver cleats.

"Mommy, look! *Tap shoes!*"

Would another parent refuse? Would another parent steer her child away? We find a size 6. I tie the silky laces. They fit just fine. "Anna's tap shoes!" she says, standing up. They're only $11.99. Would another parent refuse?

The shoes do not disappoint. The shoes offer her a completeness that will take years to understand and name. She clicks and clacks and swishes and twirls, then, through the mall, her head bent so she can watch her magic feet. "Anna's tap shoes!" she exclaims on the downbeat, and on the upbeat, too. It is a sight to behold. It is joy in motion, all happiness and delight spinning by Hickory Farms and Spencer's Gifts and right on through the food court, too. The surly teenager cracking gum, the cranky old man arguing with a clerk about change, the sad old lady drooping her shoulders low and lower still— everyone looks up, everyone looks to see where that *clickity clack* sound is coming from. They look and see her, a round girl in leopard and tulle and purple shades. A one-girl parade. They look and they are transported to some small better place, smile after smile, like a wave.

a stupid feud

We decided the heck with George. We decided to get our own damn sheep. This was after many hours of consideration.

Our back hill is about twenty acres wide and in some places the drop is as sudden as a cliff. When we first moved here, Alex mowed that hill with his big blue farm tractor, and we both nearly had heart attacks, him from aiming straight down like that, strapped to the tractor seat with a nylon belt, and me from just watching and wondering how it would be if he and the tractor ended up tumbling into the kitchen.

"So *you're* the guy who mowed that hill," neighbor farmers would say to Alex in the hardware store. Apparently, news that someone had actually taken a tractor to that cliff had hit the old-time farmer circuit as a piece of lore no one was sure was true or not.

"Yup," Alex would reply, all proud and trying to sound farmer-like. But in time he came to understand why everyone was so impressed. (*"That dude is nuts. . . ."*)

George was the one who offered to help. He pulled Alex aside. He said, "Listen, buddy." He said, "You're going to kill yourself." Then one day he came up the road with about a hundred of his sheep following behind, and he opened our gate and shooed the sheep in.

The sheep ate the grass, and they fertilized it, and they required nothing of us, not even a thank-you. Summer after summer, with George lending us those sheep for a few months, we had a back hill that came to resemble a smooth golf course, albeit crazily steep.

George accepted no money for this service and we came to understand that it was rude to even offer. This was just a neighbor-to-neighbor thing.

Then the silent feud started and no sheep came. We sat and wondered why George had stopped talking to us and if we were supposed to do something about it and if so, what that might be.

Meantime the grass grew, as Alex watched and got worried and woeful, thinking about what he was going to have to do. I said let's not mow the hill. I said let's just regard that growing vegetation as a very young forest to admire and accept. He said no, he would have to mow it. It was the right thing to do; it was a matter of stewardship and honor, a farmer keeping his fields clean and healthy. He started eating a lot of ice cream in anticipation of taking the tractor up there. The sugar from the ice cream kept him up at night. He'd finally fall asleep and wake up with a headache.

I said maybe he should just go over and make up with George, so we could get the sheep back. He said how can you make up with someone when you don't even know what you're fighting over? He said he wanted none of it. He said if whatever we did was really that bad then why didn't George just come over and confront us with it?

"True," I said.

We decided the heck with George. We decided to get our own damn sheep to eat the grass on our terrible hill.

Now, I have no reason to believe that children's author Laura Numeroff meant ill will when she wrote the popular book *If You Give a Pig a Pancake*. My girls love this book. Sadly, I have had to ban it from the house.

In this book, the pig on the receiving end of the pancake is not satisfied with just that. Like most of us, that pig wants syrup. Syrup leads to another request, inevitably and quite logically to another, and another; in fact, pages and pages of others that would seem to have nothing whatsoever to do with breakfast foods at all. The pig is not, I don't think, particularly greedy or even needy. No, the pig quite blithely and reasonably moves forth with her requests for tap shoes, wallpaper glue, all manner of nonsense—until finally, in the end, we are brought unavoidably and maddeningly back to her appeal for another stinkin' pancake.

Reading this story, thinking about this story, my head goes into a spastic twitch and soon enough I'll drool.

Too close to the bone. Too many of my nightmares right there in pig form. The tumbling effect of one stupid thing leading to another, the complications upon complications, the way you just want to kick that pig out of your house and start some particular sequence of your life over.

But it's too late for that. By the time you notice what's going on, it's too late.

The sheep would be Alex's project. He would become fluent in the language of ewes and rams and worming medications and ear tags and antifungal sheep foot dip.

He called Gretta, by now our official agent of animal acquisitions, and she taught him about Dorpers, a breed of sheep just now being introduced to the U.S. from South Africa. "They're *hair* sheep!" Alex reported back to me, having moved remarkably swiftly along the learning curve after just one phone call. Hair sheep, he explained, were different from the far more common wool sheep. You have to shear wool sheep, since the wool keeps growing and growing until pretty soon the poor animal is wearing the equivalent of twenty-five sweaters. The hair on hair sheep falls out in time, like human hair. So you don't have to shear them. Beginners in love with the romance of knitting scarves made from the wool of their own sheep may find the prospect of owning a hair sheep disappointing and pointless. But any sheep farmer worth his mutton knows that the labor involved in shearing a flock is the single most costly aspect of the business. There is no market in the U.S. for wool; sheep farmers are all about meat, mostly lamb. Shearing costs more than you'd ever get back selling wool.

So, hair sheep. That's the future. That's what Gretta told Alex. She was about to introduce Dorpers into her own flock and said she could get some for us, too. It was, she assured him, a good investment. Get in early, that's how it works with these designer animals. That's how it worked with llamas and that's how it worked with alpacas and that's how it worked with miniature donkeys. Those animals could fetch five thousand dollars or more when those markets hit their peak.

One Dorper ewe was at the time going for about a thousand dollars. But Gretta said we wouldn't have to spend that much. We could "breed up," get a ewe that was 75 percent Dorper and mate it with a 100 percent Dorper ram and eventually our sheep would have enough Dorper in them to be put on the official purebred registry.

Alex took in all this sheep knowledge and he took notes and he started a file folder and you could tell already he felt a sense of purpose.

So one day Gretta showed up and in the back of her pickup she had six "three-quarter Dorper" yearling ewes we bought for six hundred dollars apiece.

It made a surprising amount of good sense, although no one stopped to remark upon the fact that six ewes weren't going to eat even half our hill, which was the whole original point.

We had, that is, already given the pig her pancake.

The thing about farming is a lot of the original points get lost. You find yourself headed in a direction for one reason or another, and then another, and then a few left turns and then a right, and then one day there you are trying to coax six yearling hair sheep to go ahead and climb out of the bed of your friend's pickup truck.

Come on! Come on, little girls, come on!

They were gentle animals, white as the blossoms on the nearby petunias, and their faces carried the expressions you might imagine on very alert, and very worried, angels. They moved as one unit, each seemingly completely attuned to the nervous systems of the others. They weren't animals you would pet or even get to know. They were scared of us and preferred each other. In that way, they were our first official farm animals. We had goats and horses and a pony and a mule and chickens and a sheep raised by goats who thought herself a goat—all these were pets, animals with names that we talked to and imagined as family. But the Dorpers were livestock, an investment.

Come on! Get down, yee-hawwww!

Humans seem to instinctively make guttural noises when moving livestock. The ewes came off the truck and then we yee-hawed them into the paddock. We stood down at the barn with our hips jutted out, making noises like this, standing like farmers stand.

Soon enough, in the evolution of any new sheep farmer with six expensive ewes, there comes the realization: "Hey, we need to get ourselves a ram."

Gretta told us about a good lead she had on two "pure" Dorper rams, and she said she was going to buy one and she asked if we wanted to buy the other. We really couldn't think of a reason to say no.

When the ram came he was square with a barrel chest and he was packed tight as a linebacker and he had enormous testicles hanging down. I felt rude looking at them but couldn't seem to help myself. They looked like birthday balloons the day after. They looked like wobbly, sagging breasts. They looked painful to own. The ram wasn't shy about jumping off the back of Gretta's pickup truck. He took one whiff of the apparently ripe air and tore up the hill after our ewes. It was . . . impressive. We never actually saw the ram in the act of mating with those ewes, and for that I was and remain grateful.

Gretta said when all the ewes were pregnant they'd let the ram know. She said at that point we'd probably need to put the ram in a very strong pen or else he would run off down the road in search of more ewes.

Alex and I walked around trying to figure out where to build a very strong pen. We found a place that was perfect. Except there was no water source. We talked about just using a garden hose. Which would freeze in the winter. We talked about digging a ditch and installing a pipe.

You always think it's just one more thing. Just one more thing to do to complete this sheep/lawn-mowing project and then you can move on with your life.

If you want to be a sheep farmer and you have six expensive ewes and one expensive ram, after you figure out where to put a strong pen and how to get water to it, certainly the most important thing to talk about is what you're going to do about the coyotes. It's a significant problem in our area, especially in spring, during lambing season. Up at the hardware store, starting in March, all the conversation is always about how many lambs any particular farmer had lost to the teeth of coyotes. To protect their flocks, some of the farmers had taken to sleeping outside with shotguns.

Gretta said there was a better way.

We stood down at the barn with our hips jutted out, standing like farmers stand. We listened to Gretta and we decided okay, we'd get a livestock guardian dog to protect our investment. We really couldn't think of a reason to say no.

Alex was surprisingly gung-ho about the dog acquisition. In fact, the entire sheep enterprise seemed to delight and fascinate him. He had none of the pig-and-pancake reaction I was having; or if he did he never said anything. That was another reason I banned that book from our house, so as to protect my husband from seeing his life as a never-ending, continuously unfolding sequence of stupid events.

Now, the thing about the dog was, we were not allowed to bond with it. I worked on not bonding with it long before it arrived, as per the instructions from the breeder, who made it plain that we were *not* buying a *pet*. The breed, Maremma, originates in Italy, where for centuries these dogs have been protecting sheep and goats from predators. Like other livestock guardian dogs, Maremmas make their own decisions in the absence of a master. Engaging one in a more submissive pet role would only be to handicap it. So none of this poochie, poochie, smoochie stuff. You're supposed to just introduce yourself, your family, and then allow the dog to grow up with the livestock it will instinctively protect.

The Maremma breeder lived in South Carolina. She sent pictures when the puppies were born, with instructions on how we were *not* supposed to remark on just how achingly cute those little white fuzz balls were. She told Alex to wear the same undershirt for two days, then mail it to her, so the puppy could sleep with it; she said that was all the introduction the dog would need. Alex did what he was told. He studied the Maremma Sheepdog Club of America Code of Ethics. He went online and printed out maps to the breeder's house, then found a hotel midway back that would take dogs. He left for the two-day trip like a soldier with a mission. When he returned he looked more like a kid with a new dog, all soft and proud. I tried to snap him out of it. I said, "Guard dog! Grrrr."

He handed the leash over to me. The dog was just three months old, but already thirty-five pounds of fluff. She had a gorgeously solid cinderblock of a head, and she was white as the moon so we named her Luna. "Hello, dog," I said. "I am not bonding with you." Then I went inside to make dinner. Alex put her in a seemingly secure pen in the barn, and came inside.

I was chopping celery when I saw her outside the kitchen window, bounding with determination up and over the hill. "The dog! The dog!" I yelled. I ran outside in my slippers, up the hill, and yelled down to Alex that the dog was gone.

He went to the barn and got the ATV. I felt terrible. Terrible for him that his new dog was already gone but also, deep in a place I am not proud of, terrible for me because I knew he was going to ask me to ride on that damn ATV with him.

There's probably a clinical name for this, some fancy phobia, but I just call it "tippy issues." I get tippy issues when I am in a vehicle on a slope. Not heading up, nor heading down. I can do those fine. But sideways? The feeling of *leaning over* like that?

I become consumed with the thought of toppling over, rolling down and down and down into hell itself, and that's basically why I hyperventilate the way I do. Tippy issues.

Would that I had discovered this disorder before I found myself living on a farm made up of nothing but large lumpy hills, and before I got me a husband who so loves motorized vehicles that the sound of his revved-up four-wheel-drive ATV turns him into He-Man who wants nothing more than to strap his woman onto the back of that thing and haul her off into the tippy sunset.

"Maybe another time," is how I usually answer these invitations.

But not that day, a messy one by anyone's measure. It was dusk. It was not a pretty dusk, the fog and the rain holding the sky close. Of course I got on the ATV with Alex. Of course I did. Soon I was hanging on to He-Man's chest with my every fingernail fiber as we went bounding sideways forth and I was thinking: *tippy, tippy, tippy, tippy.* Followed by: *If this isn't true love, I don't know what is.* Followed by: *tippy, tippy, tippy, Hail Mary full of tippy, tippy, tippy.*

"Do you see that white thing over there?" he asked. "Is that her, or is that a sheep?"

"It's too dark," I said, which I'm pretty sure would have been true even if I were able to open my eyes. "We'll have to try again tomorrow."

"This is a disaster," he said.

"Well, at least we didn't bond with the dog," I said, clinging to all there was to cling to.

In the morning he headed off again and I got out of the

whole tippy deal by volunteering to make lost-dog posters. I tried to avoid saying the obvious: This lost dog was a lost cause. We knew nothing of the dog's habits; she was probably on her way home to South Carolina. We hadn't even had a chance to put a collar on her, and she'd barely gotten a chance to sniff out our place and mark it with her own scent. Alex would hear none of this. In the afternoon he left with the lost-dog posters, said he would put them up at the post office and the hardware store and anyplace else he could think of.

Alone in the house, I thought: We should have never started this whole stupid sheep enterprise. But at a time like that it's hard to tell where, exactly, the beginning of the story even is. Maybe we should never have started the whole farm enterprise. Maybe we should have bought a house in Cherry Hill, New Jersey, with an asphalt road out front and the kind of lawn people had other people come by and spray to discourage dandelions.

I was doing dishes when I saw Skippy up on the hill, staring east. Just frozen there in his posture of concern and dismay. That mule had long ago emerged the king of all our animals, and he took the responsibility seriously. Skippy was always on the lookout. I looked out. I traced his line of sight as best I could, across the fence and into the woods. And then I saw it: a large ball of white.

"The dog!" I hollered. I ran out in now my second pair of soggy slippers, up the hill, flip-flopping through the field to the edge of the woods. "The dog!" I yelled. "Skippy, you found the dog!"

"*Oh, puppy, puppy, puppy!*" I yelled in the high-pitched

squeal humans instinctively use to talk to puppies. "*You came back! Come to Mamma, sweetie.*" And "*Poochie poochie poo.*" I was crouching on my knees holding my arms out, like you do for any lost dog, even though I wasn't supposed to be doing quite this with this dog. Um. How do you get a dog to come home if you don't give it some loving to come home to?

More to the point: How do you not bond with a beautiful white dog that has come back to you after a night of running and whose coal black eyes look hungry and scared and who comes at you wagging her tail feverishly with love and apology?

"*Luna, girl! Come to Mamma! Mamma loves you, Luna girl!*"

Alone with that dog in the woods, scratching her belly and praising her and loving her, one thing I learned about myself was that I was no good at not-bonding. I was only good at bonding. Was that really such a bad thing?

When Alex drove up the driveway, he saw me up there waving my arms and he popped the trunk open and got something out and came running up the hill. I told him Skippy found her, I told him about the ball of white in the woods, I told him she was a good dog, I was breathless with glee. He was shaking his head, smiling, trying to catch up, and he was holding a large steak bone.

"You bought her a bone?" I said.

"In case she ever came back—"

"I don't think we're supposed to buy her presents," I told him. "I don't think it's in the code of ethics—"

"I bought a pork shank for her and also a hairbrush," he said.

"Oh, dear."

"Oh, well," he said.

We loved Luna. There was nothing that anybody at the Maremma Sheepdog Club of America could do about it. Alex bent down and scratched her belly and gave her the bone. I thought: Oh, look at this. I thought there should have been daisies in a nearby meadow, and a beautiful rainbow stretching across the sky. And a unicorn flying and emitting a shower of glitter. The completed picture, I thought. Here it was, a real happily-ever-after tale. The pig had her pancake and was now going to move on. Close that book. Throw that book out. All righty, then. The end.

That weekend my friend Robin came for a visit from New York. She brought her husband, David, with her, and a notebook with a list of questions written inside. Robin and David were adopting a baby from China, and they were coming to Alex and me for answers. Nearly all the questions were about bonding and how to make it happen. I remembered this one: When you're adopting a child you have a fear as real as a toothache that somehow, since the baby didn't grow in you, she isn't going to attach to you. Or, worse, you aren't going to attach to her.

Robin said that one of the things she planned to do when she got her baby in her arms was she was not going to allow anyone but herself and David to hold her until the bonding process was complete. That way, she said, the baby could avoid the confusion over just who, exactly, her real parents were.

I asked her how she would know the bonding process was complete.

"Well, I have no idea," she said. "How did you know?"

I told her that with Anna, I felt connected the moment I touched her, and with Sasha the process may have been a millisecond shorter, or longer, I couldn't remember exactly. "It was all more or less instantaneous," I said. "It's your baby. You're the mom. You bond." I told her not to worry about it, knowing that nothing I could say would quell her private fears. I told her that I thought all you really had to do was want to bond. But I was no longer sure even that much was necessary.

She looked at her notebook, seemed almost disappointed that there wasn't more to write down than that.

I told Robin about Luna, the dog Alex and I promised not to love. I told her I thought bonding was the natural order of things and the much harder job was not bonding.

I believed all of this, and still do. But that day with Robin I felt all wise and important. Then things went downhill because our second and last remaining pecky rooster made a beeline for Robin. I don't know what we're doing wrong that all our roosters end up being pecky, but I was done with roosters. We were standing down by the chicken coop and Robin was admiring the whole Green Acres theme of the place, and just out of nowhere and completely unprovoked, that rooster came charging at Robin while he puffed his chest and he started attacking her ankle.

"Oh!" Robin said. "Ouch!" She was so polite about this. She had lived her whole life in Manhattan and she had no practice with chickens and I think she thought there was something very normal and chicken-y about this attack.

There was not. Chicken beaks are like jackhammers. They hurt like hell. I had had it with the roosters of this world. I ran up to this one and kicked him like a football. "You're going to Gretta's!" I shouted, as he flew up into the sky and tumbled beak over feet, then fell to the ground with a thud. I ran after him and kicked him again. "You're going to Gretta's!" I shouted again and again in what everyone that day regarded as a full chicken fit.

Robin looked a lot more afraid of me than of the rooster. I don't know what this display did to my eloquent talk about bonding. *One false move and you're outta here.* I don't think of myself as a person who relates to others that way, but when it comes to pecky roosters this is who I am.

In the end, we didn't get the ram pen built in time. No, of course we did not. Because there never is an end to the pig-and-pancake story, no, once you open that horrible book you are stuck in an endless loop of responsibility and anguish.

One day we woke up and looked outside and counted the sheep and realized that the burly ram was gone.

We knew where it almost certainly had escaped to. Just over our fence lay the land of George's milk and honey: some five hundred ewes.

I told Alex he had to call George and tell him our ram was loose in his field.

He said, "I know."

We both sighed. We didn't want to have to deal with this.

The whole point in becoming sheep farmers was so that we wouldn't have to deal with George's anger with us, whatever it was. And now look.

"Look!" I said to Alex.

George's pickup was barreling up our driveway. There was a ram in the back.

"Oh, God," Alex groaned.

This was one of those times I was glad I had to bathe my children. I would have to stay inside and rinse their hair. Darn it, I would have to miss the duel with the neighbor.

"You have to admit it was nice of him to bring the ram back," I said to Alex. "Maybe it's a peace offering."

"Uh-huh," he said.

"Good luck," I said.

"Yeah . . ."

I rinsed extra good. Then I put in conditioner. I told the girls it was important to sometimes let conditioner stay in your hair and really get in there deep. I was hiding in the bathroom.

Alex was down by the barn with George for nearly an hour. Every time I peeked out, neither of them were flailing their arms or putting up their dukes.

When Alex finally came back in, he didn't look upset.

"You worked it all out?" I said. "Just like that?"

"We talked about how to build a ram pen," he said.

"Uh-huh."

"He said I should use cattle fence."

"Right . . ."

"And I told him we need a water source because I'm not hauling water every day—"

"*What about the feud?*"

"I don't think we're having a feud."

"What?"

"Well, he didn't say anything about it."

"Nothing?"

"He said to say hello and he said Pat's heart has been bothering her again."

Oh, my God. "These people don't speak to us for two years and then they just pick up where they left off with no explanation?"

"I don't think they were not-speaking to us," he said. "Could it be possible that we weren't speaking to them?"

I considered the option. "We're not in a feud?" I said.

"Apparently not."

Oh, God.

"He said he heard we got a livestock guardian dog."

"Did you show him? Did you introduce him to Luna?"

"He said he doesn't believe in livestock guardian dogs."

Well, that was the George I remembered and loved. George was a man with a belief system. "Did you talk about anything else?"

"Mostly just all sheep things."

"Jesus."

We may have evolved into farmers, but we were only beginning to understand farm culture. Out here, emotions run high but then just as quickly can go underground, unspoken. I suppose if you're lucky they choke on negligence. Or they might take root and grow like underground tubers, one generation to the next. It was way too soon to know which would be the case here.

"He said he was planning to ask us if we wanted him to bring sheep over this summer," Alex said. "He said we didn't have to go and get our own sheep."

I took a deep breath. After all this? After all this it turned out we never even had to get started with this stupid story? "Tell him to bring his sheep over!" I said. "Call him up and tell him right now! We don't have nearly enough to eat down the hill."

"I asked him," he said. "He said he can't do it now."

"He can't now?"

"No, because we have hair sheep."

"Yeah . . ."

"He doesn't believe in hair sheep. He doesn't want to mix."

"Oh, Lord."

"Are you okay?"

"You know what, I really need to go watch TV," I said.

I got in my pajamas. I put on *The Bachelorette.* I watched Jen weep her brains out over whether to pick Jerry or John Paul, the two men she had fallen in love with, and then in the end she didn't pick either. I considered throwing a brick at the TV, but instead I turned off the TV and the light and I put a blanket over my head, leaving only a tiny passageway—a meager but necessary invitation—for oxygen.

fever all through the night

I'm reporting live, from a cozy blue room generously appointed with trains and toy mice dressed in tutus. I'm here on a sliver of an edge of a too-small bed, but I do have this bit of quilt cover, so I'm, ouch, good. Really I am.

The rest of the bed, and the rest of my life, is taken up entirely by my daughter, a three-year-old with the heaviest and hottest head imaginable. Her head, featuring a 102-degree fever, is resting on my belly, somewhere around my spleen, I'd guess. But this is really just a guess. I don't know where my spleen is, or what, really, it even does, but at 4:05 in the morning you think about things like spleens. I am thinking that human spleens can't take this kind of sustained weight; I am really starting to think they can't.

My daughter is going to wake up any moment now, as she

has been doing all night long. She is going to wake up in a kind of dreamy panic, she is going to lift her head and say, "Where are you, Mommy? Where did you go?" And I'm going to stroke her cheek gently. I'm going to say, "I'm here, sweetie. Me and my spleen are right here." And she will drop her head, *thunk*, like a bowling ball on my belly, and fall instantly back to sleep.

The virus that has hold of her is a particularly tenacious one; the doctor said I should give it a good ten days.

"Good?" I said.

"Do what you can do," he said. "Just make her comfortable."

Ordinarily, I don't spend the night in my daughter's room. Oh, the parent police say to never sleep with your kid. But when your kid is sick, all the rules go out the window. Breaking rules is a catalyst for healing. I remember milk shakes when I was sick, I remember my mom wheeling the TV into my room. I remember no vegetables and no meat, just noodles and milk shakes and noodles.

But mostly I remember my mother's hand on my cheek. First my forehead, then one cheek, then the next, where it would rest awhile. Her cool, worried hand. The hand that said, "Oh, no! You're sick!"

The virus that has hold of my daughter is going around. Adults seem to get the two-to-three-day version; kids the seven-to-ten. So I've already been in one side and out the other of this one. A few days ago, I could barely lift my head. My fever shot to 103, and many doses of Tylenol brought it down to a still-miserable 101. I called my mother. She did what she could do, from three hundred miles away. She said, "Oh, no!" She said, "You're sick!"

My husband tried to pick up the slack. Of course, a husband is handicapped at a time like this: He is not, no matter how hard he tries, your mother. He needs instructions. "Here, like this," I said, taking his hand and placing it on my forehead, then round to one cheek, then the other. "Just come by and do this every hour or so, and I will probably survive." I was too weak to tell him about the milk shakes, the TV, the noodles. Too weak and pathetic and miserable and, underneath it all, disappointed in him for not being my mother.

A sick child and a mother. There's an electricity. Up until recently, I understood it only from the child's point of view. I understood it in my skin. I simply felt better if my mom's hand was on my cheek. I understood its absence as pure hunger.

Now, from a mother's point of view, I understand the reverse. For the mother, the sick child offers completion. The child needs what the mother has, what the mother is. She needs worry and sorrow and tenderness. The sick child makes the mother whole.

All night long, every hour at least, my daughter had been calling. So eventually, about two hours ago, I climbed into this little bed. I set myself up here, with a book and a night-light, and I've been fighting for more space and more quilt coverage, yanking and pulling as subtly as I can while she lies sleeping. I'm cold. I'm an old lady flying coach on a transatlantic flight. I'm getting a spleen-ache. And yet I'm so comfortable in this moment I could cry.

She is stirring again. She lifts her head. I can actually feel the heat move briefly away. "Where are you, Mommy?" she says, her eyes still closed. "Where did you go?"

"I'm right here, sweetie," I say, placing my hand on her forehead, then one cheek, then the other. "Me and my spleen are right here."

Thunk.

Ugh.

What strange joy.

apraxia

There came a day when Anna announced that she did not wish to be called Anna anymore.

"No?" I said.

"No," she said. "Because I am Princess Kitty Cat Butterfly."

"Princess Kitty Cat Butterfly," I said, generously. "A name of distinction."

Then she looked at Sasha. "Her name isn't Sasha," she said.

"No?" I said.

"No," she said. "Her name is Ed."

So for a while this is how it went. Sasha did not mind being called Ed, although she herself pronounced it "Et." We'd be in the grocery store and one of those grandfathers would come up to her, coochie coochie coo and say, "What is your name, sweetie?"

"Et."

"Ed!" I would chime in. "But that's not really her name; her sister changed it . . ."

Oh, never mind.

Some months after we all got used to the linguistic work involved in addressing our child as Princess Kitty Cat Butterfly, Anna had a new announcement: "I'm dropping the 'Butterfly.'"

"Okay," Alex said. "Just Princess Kitty Cat, then?"

"Yep," she said. "But my nickname is Kitty."

All of this came as some relief to Sasha, whose challenge to put together even two syllables was sometimes overwhelming. She could never say "Anna," in the first place. The sound "n" was, for her, utterly unattainable. "Anna" came out as "Alla," which is exactly how "Ellen," the name of the babysitter, came out. "I'm not Ellen!" Anna would say.

"Soddy, Kikki," Sasha would say. Translation: "I'm sorry, Kitty."

Eventually, "Kikki" proved more fun for all of us to say than "Kitty," and the new names settled on our tongues and found their rhythmic homes.

And so my girls, Kikki and Et.

You could look at the evolution of a lot of languages and I'll bet they started as simply and logically as this.

"When Sasha turns four, will she start talking right?" Anna asked one day.

It was an obvious question for a girl whose sister says "gilk" instead of "milk," no matter how many times you correct her. But it was one of the few times Anna made reference to being frustrated with Sasha's inability to speak intelligibly. Usually, Anna works as interpreter. She understands Sasha when no one else can.

"Mee zee too wow!" Sasha said in the car on the way to school one morning.

"What, sweetie?" I said.

"Mee zee *too wow*," she declared emphatically.

"Mom, she thinks the music is too loud," Anna chimed in.

Oh. And, of course.

The two spend their days together, so Anna has easily picked up Sasha-speak. The rest of us are still learning.

Lately I've been thinking I should be making a bigger deal out of Sasha's problem. I am too blasé about it. I wonder if some switch has turned off in me that keeps me from grieving over the fact that my preschooler has so little language.

Sasha chose McDonald's as the magical land of her birthday party. "Whoa!" she said, the first time we went there. And, could it be true? Six of her friends at the McDonald's PlayLand and presents and balloons all *at the same time*?

She managed to communicate this wish to me with her eyes and her broken sounds and both of her arms gripping my thigh with joy. So much of language has nothing to do with words. Perhaps this is why I'm not more worried about Sasha's speech disorder: I *forget*. Her lack of intelligible talking doesn't get in the way of my knowing her, or loving her, or enjoying her company, or laughing at her jokes. When it comes to sociability, a language disorder is a remarkably surmountable obstacle.

The party at McDonald's went off without a hitch, a dream come true enhanced with the unicorn balloons and unicorn plates and unicorn napkins we brought. We played pin-the-horn-on-the-unicorn and Sasha wore a birthday-girl tiara and for lunch she ordered cleek-en luggets and choco gilk.

When we got home I put a blindfold on her and brought her outside and when she opened her eyes there was her surprise: a small brown donkey wearing a giant red ribbon.

"Foh me?" she said.

"For you, sweetie," I said.

"My gon-key?"

"Your very own gon-key."

"Oh, I luff it . . . *so much!*"

I love the way she says "so much." It comes out with almost a Russian accent. Very emphatic. More like, Zo *mutch!* I've come to incorporate the phrase in many of my own declarations of happiness.

The donkey stood thirty-five inches tall, a registered "miniature" that was pregnant, which the donkey farmer we bought her from swore was a good thing. "Two for one!" he said. But he really didn't need to give me the hard sell. That donkey had been following me around all day while I went about the donkey farm looking for just the right surprise for Sasha. I thought a miniature donkey would be a good starter equine for her. Something just her size she could groom and feed and practice picking hooves. I wanted a white spotted one, something with some pizzazz. There were so many gorgeous little donkeys at that farm, all of them milling about and some of them munching on a round bale and a few huddled with their backs to me as if gossiping. I went from beautiful donkey to adorable donkey, trying to choose, and all the while there was this little brown, nondescript, dirty dirtbag of a donkey following me, like a little caboose. I finally faced the animal and said *"What?"* She looked up at me. She blinked. Then she tilted her head, as if questioning. It was not a pleading question, but more of a bored one. Like, "I'm ready? I've been waiting an hour?" That was pretty much that. I wouldn't get a gorgeous white spotted donkey. I would get a dumpy fat girl donkey because some things are just meant to be.

"My gon-key?" Sasha was saying. "She is my gon-key?" This was a very good reception, in my view, even better than I had hoped for. A miniature donkey had not, after all, had a chance to appear on Sasha's lifetime wish list.

"She's just your size," I said. "You can brush her, feed her, take care of her."

Sasha hugged the donkey and Alex took pictures. We walked the donkey around the yard and talked about naming her.

"Elise?" Sasha said.

"Um . . ."

"Woo yike 'Elise'?" she said.

I had nothing against the name. It was just that Sasha's every doll and every stuffed animal was named Elise. I suppose a lot of kids go through stages where they have default names like this.

"Oh, I don't know, sweetie," I said, turning to Alex, hoping for some help. "Woo yike 'Elise'?"

"Sure!" he said.

"No woo don't!" I said. "Listen, Sash, it might get confusing if your gonkey has the same name as your kitties."

She thought about that. Anna suggested other names. We worked on the chocolate theme because of the donkey's deep brown coat, eventually settling on "Choco," a character in one of our favorite adoption story books. The added benefit of the name was that it was one Sasha could actually say.

"I luff woo, Choco," she said, as she led the donkey into the barnyard. "Choco iss *my* gonkey!"

It was February and it was cold so we gave Choco some hay and then we went inside and ate pock-horn and we played Go Shish, the card game.

The thing is, my child is disabled. That's what I need to admit. We certainly don't treat her as disabled. We don't tiptoe around the issue or overcompensate with gushy praise or behave in a way that masks fear. This is not by design so much as that we really don't think of her as disabled. I don't know which came first, the not thinking or the not behaving, but I'm sure one feeds into the other. Recently I've started wondering when the benefits of that way of dealing with a disabled child lean and finally tip over into denial.

We talk like her. We say "gonkey." We say "gog." We say "gilk." We merge her language with ours.

There's a boy in her preschool class who every day wears a large train conductor's hat that sits just barely above his eyes. He hides beneath that hat, never looking at the other children, rarely participating in their play. Usually, when I drop Sasha off, I see him by himself, eyes gazing downward. When I run into his mother I wonder why she looks as content as she does. I want to say, "Your boy is not ready for school." I want to say, "There is something wrong with your son." She kisses him and tells him she loves him and happily goes away, down the hallway, and into her day.

One day I was assigned the job of "Craft Mom" for the class Christmas party and I was handing out the green and pink foam triangles and the glitter and the glue. When I came upon the boy in the train conductor's hat, he didn't grab at the goods as all the other kids did. He didn't respond at all. He sat on his hands, dropped his chin to his chest.

"Would you like to make an ornament, honey?" I said. "Would you, huh? Would you?"

He burst into terrified tears. The teacher came to his rescue, carried him off. When she came back I said I was sorry. I gave her the eyes that said, "But what is wrong with that boy?"

"He loves it here," she said with a shrug. "His mother pulled him out for a month, and he begged to come back."

So I don't know. Maybe nothing is wrong with that boy. Maybe he's just working all this out the way he needs to work it out. I look at others. I look at a girl who is pigeon-toed; they say give it time and it will correct itself. I look at a kid with a patch over one eye; the doctors are trying to get that lazy other eye working. I look at skinny kids with buck teeth and plump kids who seem to always be sweating and I look at a girl puffing her asthma medication. I think of all the ways kids grow in fits and starts, like plants with extra shoots you have to lop off or bent stems you must stake. And I think none of this is so weird, this is just the way growth happens. So Sasha has her problem and they have theirs and we all end up in the same place, taking buses to work or driving our cars or hailing cabs and trying to get through the day so we can get home at a decent hour and have a plate of spaghetti.

So much worry and fuss and people just go on becoming people, more or less.

Verbal apraxia is also called childhood apraxia of speech, and developmental apraxia of speech, and verbal dyspraxia. It bothers me that the people in charge can't seem to agree on a name. It seems to me that if you've taken on the task of fixing kids with problems planning speech, you would engender a lot more confidence if you'd call your cronies and plan your own speech better.

The key is the root word *praxis,* which means "intended movement." Stroke victims can become apraxic in speech and in fine-motor movement and in gross-motor movement, too. The brain simply loses the ability to properly sequence voluntary actions.

Verbal apraxia is a disorder of the nervous system. A child with the diagnosis of verbal apraxia can't consistently position the articulators (face, tongue, lips, jaw) for the production of speech sounds and for sequencing those sounds into syllables or words. There is nothing wrong with the muscles themselves. The child doesn't, for instance, have difficulty chewing or swallowing or sticking out her tongue at her sister. However, the area of the brain that tells the muscles how to move and what to do to make a particular sound or series of sounds is damaged or not fully developed. This makes retrieving the "motor plan" for saying a word difficult.

Even though the child knows what she wants to say, she cannot say it correctly on command. Sometimes she can't even begin. Either the wrong sound comes out, or many sounds are left out all together. The motor plan is simply not accessible. These errors are not under the child's voluntary control, so she typically can't correct them, even when trying her hardest. Frequently, a child will be able to produce a sound or word at one time and not be able to say it again when she wants to.

Kids don't grow out of this, in the way they might pigeon-toes or a crippling shyness. Intensive speech therapy, at least three times a week, is necessary for anything approaching success. It's not a quick fix. Most apraxic children will be in therapy at least two years and sometimes significantly longer. The reason it takes so long is because a lot of the patterns of normal speech have to be deliberately programmed into the child's brain. This takes repetition and repetition and repetition. And all kinds of tricks the average parent would have no way of coming up with on her own. Sasha needs more than just auditory prompts to get her to make certain sounds. For her, tactile cues help. The "n" sound was completely beyond her grasp for years. "Anna" was "Alla" and "nut" was "gut" and "nose" was "gose."

One day Miss Sandy took Sasha's finger and placed it on the side of her own nose. She then said words that contained "n," encouraging her to feel the vibration. She did the same using Sasha's nose and coached and coached and coached.

"Ma! Watch this!" Sasha said, at dinner that night. She put her finger on her nose and said, "Anna," clear as day.

For months every "n" word required her to stop and think and repeat the trick with her finger. Eventually, she could do it with no finger at all.

This is the way it has gone, one sound at a time and one sequence at a time and if you were to stop and look at the whole picture you would feel like an ancient Egyptian standing by a pile of rocks with some pharaoh standing over you with a drawing of a giant pyramid saying, "Here. Now build me one of these."

But normally I don't feel like that. Perhaps feeling like that is a more honest dealing with the disability.

Recently, I find myself reading everything I can get my hands on about apraxia. I think being a three-year-old who can't talk isn't such a burden but being a four-year-old who can't talk is starting to get knotty. I read some parents reporting that super-high doses of omega-3 and omega-6 fatty acids have brought the gift of speech to their apraxic kids. I think how desperate and pathetic it is to believe in miracles, in one breath, and in the next find myself calling Alex at work and asking him to stop at GNC for a bottle.

They don't know what causes apraxia, but some people say brain damage and some would say the orphanage did it. Or the ghost-mother who left her on the steps of that pharmacy. Or just the combination of so much hardship for such a tiny baby.

Nobody knows and no one will ever know, so I don't see the point of concocting stories, although the truth is it takes a lot more energy to stop myself from concocting. For the worried parent the imagination is always a bully to tame, and for the parent who fears her child has been victimized: look out. At times I feel an anger toward the orphanage workers, toward all the ghosts, that turns into brittle, hot rage. But I have no characters with which to begin to invent a plot. Not one. To make them up is to invent tragedy. To invent! Discipline is the only way I've learned to shut down the imagination, to walk away from it, the voice of cool restraint, like a buddy yanking his friend away from the clenches of the cruel heckler. Just walk away. *Walk away.*

It's not that I'm against fighting. It's just that there's no one there to fight. No one from Sasha's earliest days but spirits in the wind. If I throw my punches into the air, scream at what I imagine is left of their scent, go militant for the sake of my child, I turn my child into a victim. I set a stage featuring poor Sasha, the pathetic little orphan with the sad story and the malnourished body and the bald head and now look at her, she can't even talk.

Poor Sasha.

At four years old, she is anything but that character. She has no sense of herself as some sorry object of pity. She is, simply, Sasha. A popular kid with a ready laugh and two best friends and a sister and a gonkey.

I'm trying to figure out whether or not I should sign us up for China school again next year. We flunked out last year. That was a shame. I was giddy with love and goodness and multicultural awareness that hot September Sunday when we climbed the concrete steps into the community college.

What a thrill it was to walk into that basement registration room filled with people from China. All ages, men, women, kids. Hearing their excited chatter, the urgent utterances of a language I could not understand, all that dark hair and those almond eyes and those cheekbones jutting out like windowsills. All of it. It made my heart pound with a nostalgia for the stinky Guangdong airport, the crowd, the luggage carts bashing into unsuspecting ankles, Alex wrapping duct tape around our duffel bag brimming with souvenirs. A baby on my hip. Leaving home. Going to America. Going home.

Standing in that community college basement, I wondered if my girls felt anything, any link at all. Did they remember these eyes and these cheeks and these sounds? Was any of this familiar?

"Girls, look at all the Chinese people!" I said, stupidly. Perhaps if I gave them a boost, they would recognize something of themselves in these people.

But: nothing. Anna was coloring in her Care Bears coloring book and Sasha was intent on biting hard enough to get into the Tootsie part of her Tootsie Pop.

Well, okay. One of the reasons I signed us up for Chinese school was so that, someday, if my daughters ever wanted some of their Chinese-ness, they would have access.

This is something a lot of people who adopt from China do, some more, some less. I'm one of the less. At least so far. I'm not sure where to stand on this one, how to encourage without forcing, where the line between treading gingerly stops and turns into avoidance. When we first came home with Anna, we took her to a Chinese New Year party hosted by a group of parents with kids from China. All at once a drum sounded and out popped a giant dragon with a giant head and it began to dance around the banquet hall. Anna wasn't the only child to scream in fear, but she may have been the loudest and was certainly the least consolable. We took her out of the room and huddled with her behind the lobby door where she could at least peek at the dragon if she wanted to, but she reached in fear for the outdoors with pleading arms and tears anyone would understand, so we left.

China school was a class for kids—you had to be at least three to enroll—with their parents, which Alex and I thought was perfect. In our family we speak of China as a shared family heritage. We adopted it when we adopted our girls. Learning the language together would be a symbolic expression of that, as well as a literal one.

So there we sat in school together, Mom, Dad, Kikki, and Et, the whole family seated in Room 116. This, I figured, would be a beautiful family experience.

"Put the desk down," I said to Sasha, who was only just discovering the thrill of opening and closing a community college desk, that hinge mechanism particularly terrific.

"Yook!" she said. "Gum!" Many colors of gum, in fact, under that desk, some still ripe enough for Sasha to poke her fingers into.

"Put. The. Desk. Down."

The teacher, an energetic woman with square shoulders,

greeted the class quickly and launched immediately into the day's lesson and soon enough marched up to Anna and said, "Zhe shi shenme?" while pointing to her nose.

Anna, who was busy drawing cats, looked at me as if she was about to cry. "Zhe shi shenme?" the teacher said again. The question, I'm pretty sure, meant, "What is this?" In a stroke of genius, or because the little boy next to me had just responded to this drill with success, I spoke on behalf of my daughter when I said, "Zhe shi bizi."

"*Pizza?*" the teacher said, turning to the class. "Does my nose look like a pizza?"

But I didn't say "pizza," I said "bizi," with a soft "b" and the final "i" going up in tone, just as she had said it. She said it again. "Bizi," I mimicked.

"No, not a pizza!" she shouted, to the continued delight of the twenty-five people gathered there that day. "This is a *language* class," she then reminded us. "Everyone here has to have pronunciation! Also, everyone here has to respect the teacher otherwise the teacher get very, very upset, okay?"

"Okay," Alex said, as if to apologize for the entire family. She turned to him. "Zhe shi shenme?" she said, pointing to her eye.

"Um," he said. "Hong?"

She paused, pursed her lips, refusing to even register that answer, then moved on to the girl with the long red hair raising her hand eagerly. "Zhe shi yanjing!" the girl said perfectly.

"I think you called her eye a rainbow," I told Alex.

Right-o. So we were the dolt family. I kept thinking there must have been more of a *beginner* beginner class, but when I checked the registration form to see what was going on in

Room 115, I saw this was it. The class for three-year-olds was as beginner as it got.

"Sasha! Get your fingers out of the gum! Put. The. Desk. Down."

In our defense, many of the people in the class had taken this beginner course two and three times before, so the fact that we were so very far in the dark in hour one of day one of a semester-long course should not have been so terribly discouraging. And so what if Sasha got nothing out of this beyond a little family bonding with Chinese language going on in the background? And the fact of the matter was that I was proud of Anna for already learning a tremendous lesson in self-control in that she was not, as she repeatedly requested, just going at that giant green chalkboard with those giant sticks of chalk with which she could draw giant cats.

So, this was fine. This was a beautiful family experience, all right. I listened to the music of the class counting from one to twenty in Chinese, absorbing the wonder, relaxing into the mystery. Then, in one swift motion, Sasha escaped from her desk, darted up to the teacher with a page of scribble she had ripped out of her notebook. "Teacher!" she was shouting, although it came out, "Tee-teetch!" "A present!" she was saying, although it came out, "A prize!" Alex took off after her, and then Anna after Alex, but Anna tripped over the foot of a man in the middle row and landed right on her bizi, which has always had a tendency to bleed, and so I waited.

It's hard to know when, exactly, to proclaim a beautiful family experience a disaster, but this does seem to be their way. A beautiful family experience is a snapshot of hope. As if obeying a call for family unity, you pack that picnic and go to that beach, only to find those horrible green flies, but you did think to bring bug spray so you spray the bug spray, but it coats the croissants, and then one of the kids has to go to the bathroom, and then the other one does, and then that luscious mimosa you drank just leaves you caving into a most miserable need for a nap.

"Oh, well," I said to Alex, after he called the teacher's ear a skirt. "So we bond over our shared stupidity. It's still *bonding*."

"Look, we are not going to go down without a fight," he said, vowing on behalf of the entire dolt family to be in charge of homework.

We lasted clear into the end of October. Sunday after Sunday we went through this. Anna drew a lot of cats, but somehow absorbed everything; she learned to count from one to one hundred in Chinese and at dinner would drill her dolt mother and dolt father. She's going to grow up a scholar, the type who can glance at her notes once and ace the test. Sasha went along for the ride happily enough, and if I plied her with enough candy, I could get her to sit through an entire class. Plus, she was promised doughnuts at break.

When I started hearing myself yelling at my girls to turn around and pay attention, to sit up and stop throwing their papers on the floor, when I found myself restricting all use of crayons and markers during Chinese class because-you-girls-are-not-paying-attention, and if-they-did-not-listen-to-what-the-teacher-was-saying-they-would-*get-no-doughnuts*—that was when I knew.

The leaves had fallen and the yellow jackets were hiding inside the stone wall and one Sunday morning Anna finally said please, she didn't want to go to Chinese school; she wanted to stay home and draw chickens. Sasha cheered with the news that we were going to stay home and maybe make apple cider and carve a pumpkin. We had other things to do besides just learn Chinese. We had church and we had each other and we had a gonkey to feed and there was football on TV.

I think we'll go back to Chinese school again next year. Maybe the girls will be ready, or more ready, or maybe we'll end up quitting again in favor of piano lessons. I don't know how to do this, but I don't think force-feeding is how. Exposure without expectation, that's what I want. Anything more is to oblige, demand, slap into an obedience that stinks of apology.

I don't want to apologize to my girls for taking them out of China, a homeland that was not, in the end, a home. I don't want them to grow up apologizing for leaving, as if that crowded country gave them any choice. A lot of people seem to want to romanticize this situation, dressing their girls in Chinese silks and taking them to the mall for professional photographs to hand out. Maybe that's good. I don't know. Maybe that's better than just walking around as a woman who finds herself awakening in fits and starts with a stubborn rage. *How dare you leave these girls to fend for themselves, even for a second. How dare you! What is the matter with you people?* Discipline keeps me from going any further. Discipline and a duty to protect that runs so deep I know it in my toes.

Look: My girls are fine. My girls are home. My girls are part of a family. We are Mom and Dad and Kikki and Et. We are yellow jackets hiding in the stone wall. We have our reasons.

fossil

"It's always a leap of faith to infer behavior from fossils," the paleontologist said. I'm guessing he had to say that because everyone was inferring behavior from the fossil. I saw a picture of it in a magazine and felt depressed for days. The fossil was found in Liaoning in northeastern China and at its center is an adult Psittacosaurus, a small, squat dinosaur with a parrotlike beak that lived 125 million years ago. The skeleton is curled around those of thirty-four babies, each about the size of a Chihuahua. The babies are crowded together with their legs tucked underneath them and their heads raised, indicating that they were watching as their impending doom came to pass. It could have been a flood or a volcano or some other sudden act they couldn't escape. Or maybe the group was hiding from a predator and the mother was holding her babies tight as they all watched the predator pass. They were about to breathe a sigh of relief, but then, in one loud boom, a mud slide happened and in an instant buried the whole family alive.

You can make up endless stories that fit the picture, but the one thing I can't escape is the mother's futile attempt to protect. Millions of years have passed and here I sit, feeling an ache I believe must be hers. My bones come from her dust, brittle under the weight of her same problems, one more mother trying to figure out how to do the right thing, if her babies are eating enough, or too much, if she's got them well enough socialized, if she's giving them all equal time.

One more mother. We do everything we think is right—except when we're too damn tired to think at all. Now and again we find ourselves screaming into the wind, words never intended for the child but there they are, stinging, sticking. We are quick to clean up, lick with the guilty tongue that shames us. But that is the exception. Really the exception!

We are sanctuaries, designed as houses to protect our babies, no matter how stupidly. Not long ago in this current millennium I was in a department store when a guy came running into the shoe department and tackled another guy and the two wrestled on the floor while display shoes flew. The one on top—he must have been a cop—had a gun in a holster. That really was quite enough for me. Instinctively, I threw my coat on my girls' heads (*I threw my coat on their heads?*) and I shoved them forcefully into the back storage area where there were stacks of shoe boxes high above us, and we kept running until I saw an exit door that warned that it was for EMERGENCY USE ONLY and I didn't care. I crashed my body into the door, tripping the

alarm, a bell, a very loud bell, and I didn't care. We stood outside panting in the winter air. Safe. I didn't care about anything
else. Maybe I overreacted, but my girls were safe, so I truly did
not mind that I had to fill out a false alarm report with that fire
chief who showed up.

Now I imagine a big earthquake happening somewhere in
the middle of that story and 125 million years later they find us
fossilized, a woman with her coat over her kids' heads lying on
top of a bed of shoes, and the paleontologist is warning against
inferring behavior from the fossil, but some mother takes one
look at it and figures it out instantly.

Now they're saying we should relax more. It's in my *Newsweek*
this week, right there on the cover. "The Myth of the Perfect
Mother: Why It Drives Real Women Crazy." There's a photo
of a woman with a baby in her lap and she has all kinds of extra
arms bearing the weight of a soccer ball and a pan of bacon and
a telephone, the image intended to say exactly what so many of
us are saying: This Is Ridiculous. We're over-parenting. We've
turned into high-intensity moms because our friends are high-
intensity moms and this race toward perfect parenting is driving us mad. I tore into this magazine one night when I was
down in the dumps because I forgot, just completely forgot,
that I was in charge of the game for Sasha's Valentine's Day
party at her preschool. Worse, I got to school that day feeling so
damn proud of myself because I had remembered that she was
supposed to decorate a shoe box and bring it in so all the kids
could put their valentines in it. So I strode into school like

Cocky Mother with my shoe box wrapped in red paper with kitty stickers on it. Then I got to her room only to discover that all the other mothers had also remembered, but their boxes were bigger than mine. And more elaborate. One girl had a castle with a drawbridge and gumdrops on top. One boy had a volcano with candy worms on it. These were . . . valentine's boxes? Yes, they were. You put the valentines in the top of the volcano and inside the drawbridge.

I stood there with my little shoe box. So pathetic. So sad. Poor Sasha, having an underachieving mom like me. I kissed her and said, "Have fun at your party," and went home and ate Doritos. Later, when Sasha got home with her loot, it became clear that the valentines that she and I had so lovingly prepared the night before—a little card with a lollipop attached—were duds. Other kid offerings included whole bags filled not only with candy but also with pencils and puzzles and little stuffed toys. Bags and bags of this stuff—none of which fit in Sasha's little shoe box. The teacher had donated to her cause, giving her a shopping bag to carry her loot home in. So, I understood, finally, why the other kids' boxes were so big. And now I wouldn't make that mistake again. I figured next year I'd use a beer case and I'd make it into a unicorn head or maybe a treasure box with fiber-optic rainbow lights spewing forth.

I was thinking this through. I was planning ahead, berating myself for not getting it together. I was about to throw Sasha's stupid little shoe box in the trash when the phone rang and it was the homeroom mother saying they missed me today, didn't I know I was supposed to bring in a game for the Valentine's party?

"Oh, God," I said. "I forgot." I forgot! I had no excuse for forgetting. I was, what, too busy taping lollipops onto those pathetic little cards?

So, I got an F for Valentine's Day. Or maybe a D-. The really sad part is I walked in that day feeling like an A.

The really, *really* sad part is this has happened to me numerous times with my girls, at picnics with other moms who think to bring tablecloths and fondue pots filled with chocolate for dipping strawberries in—and there I was feeling so proud I thought to bring pretzels—at birthday parties with other moms who think to make doll clothes featuring swatches from the clothes of the birthday girl's baby wear—and here I was so proud I thought to cleverly wrap the Barbie in Barbie paper. On and on and on, the failures pile high until I wonder why I ever got into this mom gig in the first place, seeing as I'm such a flop.

So of course I tore into that *Newsweek*. How comforting it was to find kindred souls and to know there may be so many of us we had mass-market potential.

I think of "us" as the first post–baby boom generation, girls born between 1958 and the early 1970s, who came of age politically in the Carter, Reagan and Bush I years. We are, in many ways, a blessed group. Most of the major battles of the women's movement were fought—and won—in our early childhood. Unlike the baby boomers before us, who protested and marched and shouted their way from college into adulthood, we were a strikingly apolitical group, way more caught up in our own self-perfection as we came of age, than in working to create a more perfect world. Good daughters of the Reagan Revolution, we disdained social activism and cultivated our own gardens with a kind of muscle-bound, tightly wound, uber-achieving, all-encompassing, never-failing self-control that passed, in the 1980s, for female empowerment.

We saw ourselves as winners. We'd been bred, from the earliest age, for competition. Our schools had given us co-ed gym and wood-working shop, and had told us never to let the boys drown out our voices in class. Often enough, we'd done better than they had in school. Even in science and math. And our passage into adulthood was marked by growing numbers of women in the professions. We believed that we could climb as high as we wanted to go, and would grow into the adults we dreamed we could be. Other outcomes—like the chance that children wouldn't quite fit into this picture—never even entered our minds.

So wrote Judith Warner, author of *Perfect Madness*, excerpted in that *Newsweek* issue. It was stunning. To read about yourself so explicitly and perfectly is to be jolted into a kind of awareness that you exist outside of your own daily slogging from here to there. You are part of a greater whole. One of those fish in a school of fish that goes on swimming until one of you turns so you all turn; here you thought you had choices but it turns out the whole lot of you functions as one organism going with the flow of a time and a place and a set of influences and a history simply living itself out.

It makes me mad that when I was younger, busily delaying motherhood, that I wasn't stronger, wasn't the great killer whale I thought myself to be. That young woman I was in grad school, trying to become perfect, running up the hill in Frick Park one hour each day, eating nothing all day but an apple and a piece of toast, writing stories and rewriting them and rewriting them, hiding from the world until I got myself perfect—I was special! I was a uniquely neurotic young thing terrified of love, too engaged with life to bother signing up for the tired grown-up world of marriage and babies. *Special!*

No. It turns out, no. That's not who I was. I was a product of a trend toward "muscle-bound, tightly wound, uber-achieving, all-encompassing, never-failing self-control that passed, in the 1980s, for female empowerment." A cliché. I may as well have been a character in a movie, Jennifer Beals in *Flashdance*, a welder/would-be ballerina sweating bullets to a pop tune. *She's a maniac, a maniac on the floor/And she's dancing like she's never danced before.*

But what of my suffering? What of the anxiety that forced me to run up steeper and steeper hills until I blew out my knees, the refusal to eat, the ups and the downs I never really could drown in wine, the rage against my church, the angry letters to the therapists who, if they could have just helped me pinpoint the problem, I'm sure I could have fixed it. *What was the problem?*

Come to think of it, I got my hair permed like Jennifer Beals in 1983. I lived in Pittsburgh, where the movie was set, and where I embraced the whole rusty steel vibe, like she did, and I even started riding my bike over the massive steel bridges that spanned the rivers, just like she did. All of us started wearing our sweatshirts off the shoulder that year, and suddenly we discovered leg warmers. We were all in our twenties, in our prime baby-making years, and yet none of us ever spoke about having babies, if we ever even allowed ourselves to think about it at all.

Didn't I see this then? Didn't I know I was a cliché?

Of course, clichés get a bad rap. There is nothing so sinful about being one. It's all in the recognition. Right now I am a tidy-fat-girl cliché. I am a mother at school with a substandard Valentine's Day box. Those other mothers are setting impossible standards. I lie awake at night worrying that I'll never measure up. In fact, worry has become my entire motherhood theme. Lately, I sit around worrying about how much I worry. One day I decide it's too much and then the next it's not enough. It's probably too much. One little cough and I think it's time to rush the kid to the emergency room. One time I was giving Anna some liquid Advil and I turned around to get something and Anna knocked the bottle over and it spilled all over the counter but I couldn't be 100 percent certain that she hadn't actually drunk a good portion of the bottle so I called Poison Control and they told me to call 911 so pretty soon the ambulance was pulling up and the EMT guys came in and we all stood there talking about whether or not to pump my two-year-old's stomach. (We didn't.)

Alex says I worry too much and I know he's right. I think about that dinosaur and I don't think her worrying ended up doing her any good. I think about the image of that fossil and why it haunts me and the only thing that helps is to think of the alternative. Imagine all those thirty-four Chihuahua-sized babies crowded together with their legs tucked underneath them and their heads raised, and imagine no mother in the picture, no protector for them to huddle toward as the darkness came.

That's a picture of tragedy. The other is a picture of love.

If I wake up tonight worrying about all the baby dinosaurs that died without their mothers there to protect them, I'm really going to start worrying about myself.

"Perseverate" is a word I grew up using because my sister

Claire was often said to be "perseverating again." She would get stuck on whether or not the cat was eating enough and if my mother was off somewhere getting sucked up by a tornado. Then when she hit her twenties and sank into a temporary but severe depression, her worry blossomed into a full-blown obsessive-compulsive disorder. She was off being Jennifer Beals in Boston while I was being her in Pittsburgh. She was trying to become a perfect physical therapist with all the advanced degrees and she got so advanced there was nowhere left to go but medical school so that's what she did.

We'd be home for Christmas and we'd be at a party and she'd turn to me and say we had to go home because she couldn't remember if she turned the curling iron off. Before we'd leave the house, she had to check the stove many, many times because she wasn't able to fully convince herself that it was turned off. Fortunately, even in her depression, she had a good humor about this and we could make it into a game.

Having babies was the one giant act that cured Claire's depression and all its attendant wacky behaviors. Sometimes denied fulfillment is just denied fulfillment. This isn't to say that she is not now a mother who worries, and quite a lot. She will always be a worrier. But the crazy person she turned into, the young woman obsessively washing her hands, that person went away when the babies came. Just: went away.

Claire needed to be a mom. She would whine about it during those childless years when her despair was so acute. She would wail and moan. It was hard to imagine the whole mess could be solved magically with a quick fix of any kind. It was hard to believe that the one solution she was offering up was anything but wishful thinking. But apparently she'd had it right all along. She needed to be a mom.

I did, too. I just never talked about it. And I didn't have obvious weird behaviors popping out. I mean, it was acceptable to be a runner who could run the steepest hills. It was acceptable to be too skinny, as long as you didn't go too far overboard. My suffering was internal. I hid inside my perfect little house and worked at making myself perfect and I ate one apple and one piece of toast per day and I washed away the noise in my head with cheap chablis.

I needed to be a mom. In every agonizing way. In a way approaching madness. I would have traded my life to become a fossil preserved for all time in the act of supreme mothering. I would have traded it in a second. In a way approaching madness.

Claire and I were exactly the same in those ways, as are probably a lot of ex-Jennifer Bealses now obsessing over Valentine's Day boxes. I don't know if the women with the better boxes are doing better, or doing worse.

Should my daughters know that their simple existence was the thing that healed me? Should I tell them this? Would it be a compliment? I suspect it would only be a burden.

They have enough to worry about. Last night Anna got her first loose tooth. It sent her into a panic. I explained and explained about teeth falling out, and of course about the tooth fairy, all to no avail. She cried herself to sleep with a cup balanced under her chin, to catch that crazy tooth.

holy mary, mother of god

I was having trouble breathing. I was trying to . . . catch up.
Here it was, the single most important announcement to hit
our family since, well, forever, and he *forgot* to tell me?

"Well, when did you find out?" I asked him.

"A few days ago," he said, calmly smearing butter on his potatoes. We were having a late dinner. The kids were already in
bed. He chose this as the moment to fork over the news: when
he was dropping Anna off at kindergarten one morning, the
teacher informed him that Anna had been selected to play
Mary in the school Christmas pageant.

"Mary!" I said. "Oh my God, does Anna know this?"

"Well, she was standing right there when Mrs. Gagich told
me," he said.

And she didn't tell me either? *"What is the matter with you people?"* I said.

"Us?" he said.

I was hyperventilating. Mary! My soul was pulsating with spasms of joy. I was being transported to an exalted state—the Mother of God!—while Mr. Mashed Potatoes over there was staring blankly. "Honey," I said, *"Mary?"*

"Yeah," he brayed.

I reached inward and found something resembling forgiveness. "You didn't grow up in Christmas pageant culture," I said, referring to the fact that he is Jewish. "You don't understand how big this is."

"Mary," he said, "was Jewish."

Oh, this was no time for smarty-pants talk. "Our daughter is going to be the star of the show!" I said.

"I thought Jesus was the star," he said.

I reiterated my smarty-pants line. I asked him to please help me figure out just how it was they chose our child for this role. Her beauty? Intelligence? Some obvious grace? Perhaps it was the work of the Holy Spirit!

"I figured they gave it to her because it's the one part that doesn't have any lines," he said, referring to Anna's famously shy demeanor. "It's probably the only way they could be sure she would participate."

I hung my head, held on to the bridge of my nose as if for dear sanity. I did not know where to begin. Sheep, okay, sheep have no lines. Donkeys have no lines. The North Star guiding the shepherds (who hardly have any lines) may have attitude—

but no lines. You could stuff that manger full of any number of kindergartners with no lines. But there was only *one* Mary. *The* Mary.

"Mary!" I said. I had to make some calls. I had to spread the word. I had to find out who was in charge of wardrobe. I needed to talk to the casting director and compliment him or her on the divine elegance of the decision to put my child in this role.

I did quick calculations in my head, figuring how many other potential Marys she beat out. Three kindergarten classes of twenty kids, and about half of the total were girls, so *thirty*! Wow! What's a stage mother to do? How would I talk to the other mothers whose children were cast as mere angels? And what was I going to *wear* to the big show? I would need a mink stole, some boots with high heels, a long, thin cigarette holder. I would insist on no more photos, please!

The next morning I greeted Anna with a smile. "Mary!" I said gleefully. "Why didn't you tell me?" She did not immediately understand the reference. "Honey, *Mary?*" She smiled, finally. She said, "Anthony is going to be Joseph and we have to wear sandals."

"Aren't you excited? I mean . . . Mary!"

"I got picked to be the helper last Friday, too," she said. Right. The person in charge of juice. Why was she telling me this? What, exactly, is the matter with my family? Was this how Mama Rose felt when Gypsy was just getting started?

Mary! I had no patience for my family. I had to start wooing reviewers; I had to think about what I would do about all the agents who would surely call; I had to think about changing our phone number and I had to start both my kids wearing big hats and sunglasses.

I called every friend I could think of to tell them the news. Wendy, bless her heart, was particularly thrilled. She told me that Melanie, her daughter who attends a different kindergarten, was going to be a sheep in her pageant. I told her that was sweet and suppressed all feelings of superiority. We compared dates and it became apparent that Melanie had been cast in the *church* pageant—the big one, with grown-ups—whereas Anna's pageant was limited to her school.

Now, I love Wendy. I love Melanie. And yet I could tell right then and there that I was acquiring fangs. In my mind I weighed Mary-in-a-school-pageant versus a-sheep-in-a-church-pageant, and although I could not figure out which one won, I knew one thing: I now had to find the hideous strength to tell Wendy ours was not a *whole school* pageant, but just a kindergarten one.

I didn't, in the end, do it. I just went obnoxiously on and on about Mary. How often in my life am I going to get to do this, I reasoned, and when Wendy asked me how she might purchase tickets to the big show (*tickets?*), I told her that I thought it was sold out but I could check. (Help!)

a day at the mall

On the spur of a hot Saturday moment when we were killing time in the mall, flipping and flopping in our flip-flops and enjoying all that air conditioning, I stopped in to see if there were any available appointments at the Pedicure Junction nail salon. The girls were old enough for beauty treatments, I reasoned, and I knew the idea would sit well with my friend BK, who was due to join us, and whom I'd been more or less babysitting ever since she started her chemo. Actually, the babysitting started shortly after the diagnosis, a small "invasive ductal carcinoma" in BK's left breast that sent her spiraling.

We didn't have any prescribed mall plans so I figured after some food-court pizza we could all sit in a row and giggle together while the ladies painted our nails lipstick red and we all gossiped about underpants. To a four-year-old and a six-year-old, there is nothing funnier than the word "underpants."

I walked into Pedicure Junction and all the manicurists were young Asian women, and so naturally they beamed when they saw Anna and Sasha, throwing smiles to one another and chattering in Chinese. I was pretty sure it was Chinese, as opposed to perhaps Korean or Vietnamese, or maybe this was just wishful thinking. Every time I meet a woman of obvious Asian descent and find out she's from China, I feel happy and connected. We are long-lost sisters. We grew up on the same street. We fought in the same war. We share some anonymous link.

One of the women approached and opened the little gate leading back to the long aisle of manicurists. "Three of you?" she said with a wide smile. "Come pick your colors."

"There's another," I said, holding up four fingers. "My friend is coming."

"Sit, sit, sit," she said.

"Actually, I just want to make an appointment for a little later," I said. "When my friend gets here."

"What color?" she said.

"No, I need to wait for my friend," I said, pointing to my watch to suggest another time.

"We paint you now, your friend later."

"Um, I'd like to schedule us all *together* . . ."

But she took me by the hand and already the girls were sitting with another woman who was dazzling them with her display of glitter polish, and in no time I found that I was sitting in a big white leatherette lounge chair with a shiatsu massage mechanism working my lumbar region and my feet were soaking in a pool of invigorating bubbles. Did I say I wanted a pedicure? Did I even indicate that desire?

Oh my God, China, I thought. I forgot all about this. But this was exactly how it was in China. You never walked into a shop and simply browsed. There was no time for browsing! *Sit, sit, sit. And here, let me take your children off your hands, here's a yo-yo for them to play with, and here's my aunt she loves babies, she will play with them, sit, sit, sit, do you like this? What kind of pearls do you like? You would look good in jade. You should try on jade. Here. This one. You take this one for you and how about buy your daughter something for when she gets married someday, you should get her something just like yours. Sit, sit, sit. This is pretty. This is nice. Do you like this? I will wrap it up.*

In China I never got the sense I was getting snookered, exactly. The exchange was simply pragmatic. It's a crowded country. It's a busy place. There's not a lot of time for folderol. You're here for a reason, you want to buy something, so let's just get to it so we can all move on to what's next.

I called BK on my cell phone. "You want a manicure?" I said. "We're at the nail place outside Sears."

"Oh," she said. "That sounds good."

"You better hurry," I said. "And be thinking about what color you want."

"Huh?" she said.

"Just . . . hurry!"

Then I hung up so I could concentrate on my calves, which were experiencing a deep-tissue massage by a woman with a wide brow and skimpy jeans and little high heels. She was sitting at my feet, hovered over the shallow bath of bubbling water, and a pudgy American in the chair next to me was having the same thing done to her and she was smiling at me as if to say, *"Isn't this positively heavenly?"*

It was. And maybe if the woman doing the massaging weren't from China, but, say, from Peru or Poland or Idaho or some other place, I wouldn't have been having quite the allegiance problem I was having, but then again maybe I would. I think you have to be heavily into the "services" circuit—a person who regularly gets massages and facials and other treatments—before you can successfully block out the notion that you are a spoiled brat with enough cash to pay for this nonsense, while the person kneeling at your feet and scrubbing off your calluses and not complaining is figuring out any way she can just to get by.

"Mom, she's from China!" Anna yelled over to me about the woman applying blue sparkle polish to her nails.

"I China too!" Sasha chimed in.

This was exciting. It gave us all something to talk about. Well, it would have.

"Ni hao!" I said, over and over again, the Mandarin expression for "Hello," and the only word I could seem to pull up from our Chinese lessons at the community college.

"Ni hao!" Anna mimicked.

"They speak Chinese?" one of the women said, motioning to the girls.

"Oh, Anna can count to one hundred in Chinese!" I said to them, then to Anna, "Honey, do your counting!"

My daughter looked at me, drew the same blank I was drawing. "Can you do it for the people?" I said, and tried to get her started with the Mandarin words for "one," "two," and "three," but I couldn't seem to remember them. If I could just get her started, the numbers would roll off her tongue, I knew they would. She was really very good at this.

"Oh, how do you say 'one, two, three'?" I said to the woman at my feet. She looked at me, smiled. She spoke no English at all. "Can someone get us started?" I said to some of the other women gathered. "What is 'one, two, three' in Mandarin?"

"Thirty-five dollars," a woman at the sink said.

Huh?

"Thirty-five dollars," she said.

"Um, I'm talking about counting in Mandarin," I said. "How does it start? *Anna, don't you remember how it starts?*"

"I am going to get one hand blue and the other hand green, Mommy," she said, way too far gone into the manicure scene to care about Mandarin.

"Well, she *can* count to one hundred," I said. "You just have to get her started."

"Ahhh," said one, smiling. "Chocolate?"

Chocolate? She could see my confusion. *"No, I said she can count to one hundred in Mandarin,"* I said, raising my voice loud, like you do in nursing homes.

"Ice cream?" the woman said.

Okay, I officially had no idea what we were talking about.

I shook my head, shrugged. The women gave up on me. They began chattering to one another in Chinese, smiling much of the time, looking over at my girls, and then one of them seemed to get angry about something and a debate ensued. Arms flailing, fingers pointing, brows narrowed and lips pursed. I sat there wincing, as you might when trapped in the crossfire of another family's fight, but I didn't just stay there. No, soon I was cringing, gripped with a ridiculous paranoia. The argument could have been about the temperature of the pedicure bath water, or about towels, or about paychecks, or about a mutual friend who needed a ride home, but what I imagined in all that animated Chinese chatter was a debate about me and my girls. That's where my imagination went. They were talking about me. And *my* girls. These little girls here, who looked like them, but no, they were *my* girls. The women were commenting on what a crazy mixed-up picture this was. Of course they were. *Who is the mother here? That one? Her? The one getting her feet massaged? The bleached-blonde American in jeans and a tank top spending her Saturday flipping and flopping through the mall and dreaming of food-court pizza? Her? She's the mother of these Asian girls?*

Yeah, I'm the mother. And yeah, my girls are from China and you women working here are all from China but these are *my* girls. Girls I took away from you. No, girls you gave up. Girls I rescued. Girls who rescued me. Girls I stole?

In one unexpected moment of clarity, or maybe it was transparency, I tumbled into a nameless shame.

When I was working on my last book, about adopting Anna from China, a professor visiting the English department where

I teach asked me if I was struggling at all with the material. "Of course," I said, since writing is almost always a struggle, a miserable truth I didn't feel like descending into at the time, so I tried to remain optimistic. "But I just got a few chapters in to my editor and she liked them, so at the moment I think I'll survive." She asked me about the content of the chapters and I told her they included some of the tender moments upon first holding Anna in my arms, a section I reworked a thousand times so as to avoid making it as sappy as, in fact, it was. "It's hard to write about that kind of joy without getting all gooey and sentimental," I said. We were standing by the department mailboxes and I was sorting through my mail, throwing out all the invitations for evening lectures on dialectical approaches to pedagogy, seeing as my nights were now pretty much booked with bath time and story time and watching the girls twirl around to the beat of "Toot Toot Chugga Chugga Big Red Car."

"Oh, I don't know why she won't let you write about what you *really* want to write about," the woman said.

I looked at her blankly. Did she mean Anna or my editor? Anna was only three at the time so I assumed she meant the latter. "Yeah, I know . . ." I lied.

"No commercial publisher wants to deal with American imperialism!" she said, with a knowing chuckle, so I chuckled, too. "Or the politics of white supremacy inherent in the international adoption trade." She went on like this. "It would be so interesting to read about the ways in which you locate and manage the guilt you must on some level feel when facing up to your own complicity in such a fundamentally racist experiment."

I think I had my eyebrows way up. I think I had inhaled but the exhale wasn't coming out. There were so many things I wanted to say, not the least of which was, *"What in the name of poopie diapers are you talking about?"*

"The personal is political!" she said with a smile.

I stood there speechless. I hate this. I'm so bad at expressing anger, so lame at returning punches. When it comes to fight or flight, I'm on the first available plane. Only well after the fact do I imagine what I could have done if I had stayed for battle.

"Look," I could have said, "you can criticize my work all you want, but stay away from my kids." Or, "Hey, where do you come off talking about the ways in which I formed my family?" But that wasn't quite it, either. "What do you mean . . . *experiment?* My children are not an experiment!" Or, "Listen, sweetie, you don't get to turn my kids into a victim for your cause. Get your hands off of them! Off!"

I didn't say anything. Or, at least, anything intelligible. I think I mumbled something about being late for class and went on my way.

I had a hard time writing anything for a while after that. I walked around for months trying to untangle the attack. Here we had one brainy Caucasian female accusing another of participating in a "racist experiment," with an oblivious yet deliriously happy tutu-wearing preschooler its guinea pig and victim. This was, to me, as preposterous as accusing me of secretly sheltering space aliens in my basement. Why would I even waste time entertaining the thought? Perhaps it was the delivery, the confidence with which that woman leveled the accusation, that made it stick.

White American guilt. To be a socially responsible white American in America today is to have white American guilt. It's good to have white American guilt. It means you're a thinking person, a moral person, a person who has some awareness of the fact that you are entitled, spoiled, fat, and greedy. This was the subtext of my attacker's claim. I was busted for having no white American guilt, or certainly not enough of it. I believed that woman and I felt guilty. I hadn't had the time for white American guilt. I'd been too busy trying to find the matching lids to all those sippy cups and wondering why the sippy cup industry didn't standardize those damn things. I'd been too busy scrubbing spilled glitter out of my living room carpet and shopping at Target for some kind of craft table I could set up to save my floors from the ravages of Elmer's glue and Play-Doh chunks.

(I don't know if my attacker had kids, but I doubt it. One thing about mothers is we give each other enormous slack around almost every issue. Cleaning throw-up off one's shoulder has a supreme leveling effect.)

So, I was . . . a racist? No, I was a *dolt* racist, ignorant of my own crime. If only I had had an *awareness* of my offense, I could have written about it. I could have put it in some larger geopolitical or moral context, and thus receive from my attackers the forgiveness that comes after a show of noble guilt.

I felt like an idiot. I felt irresponsible. I felt like running away, taking my girls to a deserted island where we could duck the madness—and this is what I more or less did.

When I was a kid I learned the best thing to do when I was angry, or scared, or disgusted, was run to the neighbor's backyard where they had a little barn with a pony and some rabbits and even a goat. I'd stay there for hours just talking to the animals about how cold it was or how hot it was and how I might assist them with any of their comfort needs. Now I have a fifty-acre farm I live on and where if you don't put the chickens away at night the raccoons will come and eat them in just a few quick gulps. These are important, urgent matters that steal your attention. Anger and shame and guilt and other worldly matters get absorbed into the earth, or they dissipate into the clouds, or maybe they just hide in the soft folds of your skin.

I'm an avoider. I don't take people on. I decide they're not worth my time. I move on. I go about my life. I know I'm a good person. I don't care what anyone else thinks. I drink wine. I watch TV. I get insomnia. Then one day I'm at the mall, at the Pedicure Junction nail salon, and I've got my feet in a tub while all these Asian women around me are bickering in a language I can't understand, and there I am, with zero evidence to support the theory, but fully convinced that the conversation going on around me is about me and my girls and my crime at taking them from their homeland.

The day at the mall was at least a year after the attack from the visiting professor in the English department. A full year. And there I was wincing, listening to a language I could not understand, but wincing like some kid expecting to soon feel a punch.

My girls. Not their girls. Girls who looked like them but talked like me. Girls who brought back memories of their own childhoods, or reminded them of the cousins they left behind, or whose eyes seemed to whisper rumors, the hush-hush of babies disappeared.

My girls. And yet girls with toes that wiggle in angles utterly different from mine. A girl I call Anna who has a tough, compact body, oblivious to cold and heat, a ruggedness earned in my imagination by ancestors toiling in rice paddies, wearing hats made of bamboo and shaped like lampshades—a cliché. A cartoon I draw on the blaringly blank page of her ancestry.

And Sasha, a circus gymnast. A tiny little girl with big almond eyes and skinny arms strong as piano wire; surely she descended from a family of trapeze artists. She would have been the one they shot out of the cannon at the end of each show. The finale! She would have *loved* that! (And so I sign her up for gymnastics class at Gym Dandy's gymnastics studio. An apology?)

My girls. Girls with a history that really only begins with me. Girls taken away. Girls left behind but girls taken away. Was one of those manicurists thinking me wrong and the other setting her straight? Or perhaps the reverse was true: one was saying how laudable it was of me to take these girls from the orphanages, and the other was furious at her for not seeing my crime.

That day at the mall, I wanted to participate. I sat there in that vibrating chair getting my calves massaged and my feet scrubbed and my shame exposed, wanting to explain that there was really nothing to this picture. Really! I was just a mom and these were just my girls and we hang out at the mall and we make jokes about underpants.

Couldn't we just be that?

Tourist Trap

by Kevin Minh Allen

Middle-class wives
can't get enough of these infants.
So adoptable, adaptable,
so contractually obligated
to fit neatly in a grateful paradigm.
After their husbands hand over the check
that greases the palms of the minister of interior,
who dropkicks the orphans over the border,
these sunburnt women catch them in their gardening
   hats
and shine them on their aprons,
like so many apples in a bowl.

By the time BK arrived at the mall, my toenails were dry and my fingernails needed only a few more minutes and BK decided to forget the whole manicure idea anyway. "Let's get pizza," she said. She was wearing "Buffy," her wig. She named the wig as a way of trying to make light of the situation. She was doing better ever since the doctors started pumping her up with antidepressants. She never fought the idea of having to take pills in order to cope.

When BK got sick, we all wanted to help. It was strange because she didn't seem sick, or at least she didn't until the day they found the lump. It was sometime midway during the second season of *The Apprentice*; one morning she called me, as usual, to complain about the way they had to dub Trump's boardroom speech, only that wasn't why she was calling at all. "They found something," she said. I swear she was completely healthy up to that point, but then as more news came in, you could see her start withering, like a potted plant in October.

They told her the tumor was tiny. They said "lumpectomy." They said maybe she wouldn't even need radiation, and that she would almost certainly be spared the ravages of chemo.

After the surgery the lab results came in and the story grew considerably bleaker. Her cancer was a particularly aggressive one, and so it would require aggressive treatment. Even with that, the five-year survival rate was low enough to actually become a fact worth mentioning.

We rallied. Nancy, Beth, Chris, Wendy, friends who had helped each other through scores of boyfriend and work and home-remodeling emergencies, but never anything approaching the severity of this. BK didn't have a husband or kids; we were her family and we felt all the tugs of that responsibility. We called each other a million times. BK was spiraling down. She seemed incapable of the smallest act of helping herself. She stopped eating not as an act of defiance nor even an expression of misery but, simply, because she "forgot." It was ridiculous. None of us knew what it felt like to have cancer, but we couldn't understand BK's surrender, her utter lack of muscle when it came to the fight. We would call each other and whisper our intolerance, release it, then return to battle on her behalf. We imagined ourselves soldiers, brave and tough marines, although none of us ever found the courage to utter a phrase as scary and hideous as "five-year survival rate."

This was complicated by the fact that earlier in the year the singer Melissa Etheridge had appeared on stage at the Grammy Awards with her post-chemo bald head singing her guts out with such passion and triumph it made you half want to get cancer so you, too, could see what you were made of and display it in your own chosen artistic form. When BK's diagnosis came, we all made the Melissa Etheridge link. We told BK to use that performance as her model. We told her to be strong and be cool, like Melissa Etheridge. We told her she might even have the chance to do the world some good, like Melissa Etheridge. Having a friend with cancer was like having your own personal symbol of strength and resolve.

That she was failing to live up to this was confusing and upsetting and disappointing. *Come on, BK. Be strong. What is the matter with you? You have to fight this thing. You have to stand tall.*

In my house we have a little guest room. The walls are lemon yellow, and the ceiling is all bead-board painted glossy white, falling into steep slopes around the bed. I go there when I have the flu. It's a cocoon. It's a room that holds you in its embrace until you get good and claustrophobic. I usually come out screaming within twenty-four hours. BK never came out screaming. She would tiptoe out reluctantly, usually just to pee. Weekend after weekend she came to the house and stayed in that room, her escape. It was an odd choice, coming to my house. She had never been the farm type, wasn't the sort of person who found solace in wide-open spaces. She avoided our baby ducks, and when we bottle-fed our sweet lamb, BK faked a smile. I couldn't understand any of this. I couldn't understand a person who wasn't healed, instantly, by the sight of a baby lamb. "Or, look at the magnolia tree in bloom!" I'd say. "Look at this beautiful day!"

She would look at me with eyes full of tears. I wasn't helping. I wanted to help, but I wasn't helping. In time she became the crazy lady in our attic, a resident to avoid. I finally had to ask her if she thought coming to my place was in her best interest. She said being surrounded by family noise was the comfort. She said her own house was too quiet, no one there making noise but the cats.

One of the things I started doing was arranging outings. I just thought it had to be good to get her out of that room. And there were errands to do. And on Saturday mornings the girls had horseback-riding lessons, which BK did not want to ever attend because horses stink, so she would sleep in and then she would meet up with us afterwards, often at the mall, a place where she felt safe. She was a good little shopper. She had, in fact, already determined that while other aunts would be responsible for introducing my girls to the arts, and the equestrian life, and sports, BK would be "the aunt who taught them how to shop."

So that's how BK and I ended up at the food court in the mall that Saturday, like so many Saturdays, and this time on the heels of some manicure confusion. The girls ate their pizza and then went over to climb on the jungle gym ingeniously provided by the food-court design team. BK stared down at her pizza. I told her I was sorry about the missed manicure. She shrugged. The last thing on her mind was nail polish. She shook her head. Back and forth, looking down at her pizza. I was going to tell her about my crisis, my swirling guilt over the fact that I had no white American guilt, but somehow it all seemed so . . . privileged compared to her crisis. My friend was a drowning woman. And I was a skinny tan girl standing there wondering if my bikini made me look fat. That was the difference. She had her problem and I had mine, and that was the difference.

"I never thought I would be like this," BK finally said that afternoon. "I thought I was a fighter."

"You are a fighter!" I said. Much of my role with her had been that of boxing coach, getting her ready for the next round. "Come on, now!"

She shrugged. I reminded her once again of Melissa Etheridge's performance at the Grammys. "We should get a tape of that. You know, you need to look to her and borrow some of her strength."

"I'm *trying*," she said. "That's the thing. I'm *trying*. Don't you think I want to be a rock star instead of some scared little girl?"

We both sat on that one for a while. I think she was surprised to finally see things so clearly. "I just hate who I am in this," she said, as if this were the conclusion, the end of the story. "You know? I'm stronger than this. *I am better than this.*"

"So you're beating yourself up for being a scared little girl?" I asked.

"Yes, I am," she said. "Because I'm better than this."

I sighed. I could see in an instant that the whole Melissa Etheridge strategy had bombed.

I looked over at my girls, who were taking turns jumping off a giant rubber pig. They were not, in that moment, scared little girls, but I could recall witnessing plenty of recent fear-filled afternoons—an easier and more immediately accessible source of material than all the scared-little-girl days of my own youth. Who doesn't have a hundred chapters of those? I reminded BK of the day she had accompanied me to the girls' swimming lessons. Sasha was the little swimmer everyone wanted her to be, a fearless tumbler who would throw herself into the water, leaping like a flying squirrel off the side and landing in a belly flop. People actually applauded. Then there was Anna, sitting there on the edge dangling her toes. Over and over again the instructor pleaded with her to come in, and when she finally did it was only to wade. The instructor showed her how to put her head under water, but the most Anna could manage was to touch that water with her lips protruding into a kind of pathetic kiss. Then she would run out of the pool as if for dear life and sit again on the edge.

"Do you think we should have yelled at Anna?" I asked BK. "Do you think we should have taken her out back and given her a whuppin' for being scared?"

She smiled, shook her head no, got the point.

"You don't beat up a scared little girl for being scared," I said. *"You take care of her."*

"Yeah, I know."

She sat there nodding. I sat there nodding.

"I'm not Melissa Etheridge," BK finally said. It came out like a big exhale and an apology all in one. Even I felt the relief.

"It's okay," I told her. "It's really okay."

"I feel like I'm letting a lot of people down," she said.

"We're just all trying to figure out how to help," I said.

"Yeah."

"It's okay to be scared," I said. "It's really okay."

"I don't want to die, okay?" she said.

She sipped her soda and I curled my straw around my thumb, both of us falling into a silence stripped free of the awkwardness of before.

"You know what," she wisely said, "I don't think even Melissa Etheridge is Melissa Etheridge."

"No, probably not," I said. Fear isn't something people flaunt.

Even Melissa Etheridge isn't Melissa Etheridge. It was a good line. We used it as a mantra for much of the rest of that day, and beyond.

The thing that gets me still is how easy this is to fall into, all this vicarious living. We pick people to act out our fantasies, and we demand a certain standard. The roles are usually those of heroes or villains. (Why bother imagining anything but the good parts?) So we all wanted BK to be a tough girl rock star shouting away her cancer—and a colleague of mine at the university wanted me to be a hapless participant in some white supremacy machine. I'm sure I made for that woman the perfect idiot, a paper doll to hang horrible clothes on and watch bend and go limp under the weight of my own ignorance. And BK made for us the perfect hero, a paper doll to hang cool clothes on and watch on the stadium Jumbotron singing and writhing and sweating and believing.

Oh, well. So she wasn't that.

Oh, well.

Theory is luxury. Analysis is a dance. Survival—whether it's a cancer victim, a baby abandoned on a street corner, or a woman desperate to become a mom—isn't fancy or stylish, political or hypothetical.

BK and I agreed she should go ahead and do her cancer the BK way, and we wondered together what that way was. "There's a lot of funny stuff that happens," she said. "I haven't really allowed myself to laugh yet."

"That's a great start," I said.

We wondered together about Buffy, her wig. Was that really the BK way to do cancer? I told her I figured her as someone who would just go on ahead and be bald. "Or maybe as the baseball cap type."

"Yeah, that would be more like me," she said, and she considered whipping that wig off right then and there at the mall.

"But Buffy does look good on you," I said. "That bob is the perfect hairdo for your head."

"I *know*," she said. "I love this stupid wig. Who would have guessed?"

"I *know*," I said.

"Buffy stays," she said.

"You go, girl."

Transracial Abductees and friends will be presenting a workshop at the bi-annual Incite! Color of Violence Conference III, in New Orleans. The Color of Violence Conference is a gathering and action of women of color workers, organizers, artists, students, and activists organizing to stop the war on women of color. Our workshop, entitled Abduction Politicks: Exposing Racism in the Transnational Adoption Industry, will be on Saturday, March 12, 2005, 11:30–1:30 p.m. And we will naturally focus on Militarism, Racism, and Imperialism in the Abduction Industry. Propaganda will be given out on a first come first served basis so don't miss your chance to get your official Spring 2005 Transracial Abductee Gear!

I found this announcement on a website run by and for internationally adopted kids now all grown-up and unhappy, or, as they identify themselves, "angry pissed ungrateful little transracially abducted motherfuckers from hell." The group rejects the term *international adoption* in favor of *transracial abduction*, a slight compromise, for the sake of attracting a wider audience, over its preferred *transracist abduction*. The site offers numerous links to "abduction literature," and discussions of the ways in which the U.S. State Department is aiding abductions, as well as recommended outlets for "Resources & Revenge."

I spent a few days clicking, and reading, and clicking, exploring a way of thinking I could have never imagined on my own. It was like lifting a log in the woods and finding a whole new and strange colony of bugs; you stand there marveling at the oddly iridescent colors of those squirming insects, oohing and ahhing and saying, "Good Lord!"

I found an essay by Kim So Yung, a young woman who was born in Korea and adopted as an infant by an American couple doomed, in her eyes, by their whiteness. Her complaints were loud, angry, and numerous. She thought of her parents as racists who had abducted her, and herself as innocently and horribly complicit in their crime. "I didn't really enjoy being the object of their humanitarian efforts, and what amounted to some really twisted racist love, but that didn't matter. I was supposed to appreciate it."

The essay went on for pages in what felt to me like machine-gun fire, an attack that was brutal and unrelenting against virtually anyone who might see international adoption as anything but a crime against humanity. "Transracial abduction is a selfish 'easy out' for white people who feel upset and guilty over the effects of racism on communities of color and try to assuage their guilt by opening up their 'loving homes' to children of color 'waiting' to be abducted. This is just really pathetic."

I felt sick when I read all of this. Of course. Any mom who watches her sweet angel asleep in a bed overcrowded with Care Bears and My Little Pony paraphernalia and various stuffed creatures decorated with rainbows and sparkles—any mom sitting there and imagining her baby turning into a young woman with such rage would get sick.

I am trying to be bigger than that. I am trying to prepare. One day Anna could come to me with anger like this, and one day Sasha could scream at me for being guilty of a sin I don't even understand. It doesn't appear in the essay that Kim So Yung's mother was an evil character, or a person determined to promote one political point of view or another. I sit here thinking, Oh, honey, what could you have done differently? What could you possibly have done? I sit here with compassion I should probably feel for Kim So Yung, but I feel it for her mother.

I find myself doing what my mother did, when I came at her with some crisis that didn't fit into her scheme of knowing me, didn't meet her expectations of who I should be: I belittle that girl. I think: this is just a stage. I think: it's kind of cute, when you think about it. Good for Kim So Yung, whose name may be real or may be the play on words that neatly fits my theory. Youth is all about rage. Good for her for articulating it. You should do something with your rage, channel it into something productive.

I hope by the time I am the mother of young adults, of women with wild thoughts all their own, I hope by then I have turned into a mother with more skills and more depth than this. Mothers grow, or at least they can. Mothers can grow, too.

Right now I can't imagine my Care Bear girls growing up to be young women with Kim So Yung's anger. I can't imagine who I'll be in the face of daughters who find themselves mired in that sort of mud. I certainly can't imagine myself heroic and tolerant, applauding, a mom cheering on her children for growing into fully independent, free-thinking adults.

I can't imagine any of it because I can't see past my nose. My story is all immediate foreground, the business of motherhood yanking me this way and that, over and over again until I flop into bed each night. The backdrop is a simple sketch I drew long ago and have little time or need to revisit. I adopted my girls because I was a mom in need of children, and they were children in need of a mom. My story is about family and fulfillment. It really isn't any more complicated than that.

When I adopted my girls, I became a part of their history, and they became a part of mine. We inhabit this story together, hapless citizens muddling through. We go about our days bumping into people who may or may not have something to say about us, a manicurist, a lady at a mailbox, an angry teenager online; anybody can talk, anybody can theorize, anybody can argue. But in the end it's just us. A mom and two girls getting their nails polished, making jokes about underpants. The personal is political, I know, but that doesn't mean every onlooker gets a vote.

Listen, girls: for now, at least, it's just us. I'm your mother and I make the rules and this is how I do things. So say your prayers, thank God for now, and put away the chickens.

nights at the opera

And deep in the Grickle-grass, some people say,
if you look deep enough you can still see, today,
where the Lorax once stood
just as long as it could
before somebody lifted the Lorax away.

He's at it again, reading a bedtime story to the girls. He sits on the flowered couch, Anna curled up on one side of him and Sasha on the other. Mr. Popular. For weeks now the featured performance has been Dr. Seuss's *The Lorax.* His voice goes from smooth and sweet, to geeky and nervous, to an outright bellow that seems to disturb even our fish.

And so goes the evening noise in our house, every night an opera.

I do the dishes, trying to feel useful. The last time I tried to read *The Lorax* (but only because he was out of town), I got corrected a lot. Those little brown guys were Bar-ba-*loots*, not *Bar*-ba-loots, my girls assured me. And I used the *gluppity-glupp* sound effect when I should have used *schloppity-schlopp.* There were all sorts of problems.

Oh, well. I've long since stopped trying to compete. Really, we're in different leagues. When I first started reading books to my children, I felt I could deliver a very competent, albeit straight-ahead *Goodnight Moon*. Then Mr. Popular stepped in with his multimedia approach, and story time in our house became something else entirely.

At the moment, they're at the page where the Humming-Fish first appear. I know this because all three of them have broken into the "Hmm hmm hmm" song he invented for the occasion.

Standing here with my dishpan hands, I'm thinking how peculiar it is to watch your husband morph into a father. The man you knew one way becomes bigger, more complicated. Why does my husband put so much of himself into reading to our girls? It's not even necessary. This is one thing a parent doesn't have to be all that good at. Most of the time the stories speak for themselves, and any competent narrator will do. In extreme circumstances, you can yawn your way through a story; you can even cheat and skip pages; you don't have a boss over you to impress or a ticket-paying audience that might give you bad reviews, no, the audience you have is completely fulfilled just in your act of showing up. I suppose the only reason to give reading a book your all, to give it the old operatic effect, is: love.

"Mister!" he said with a sawdusty sneeze,
"I am the Lorax. I speak for the trees."

The Lorax is an unabashed environmentalist's plea; the bad guy (who redeems himself with regret) keeps cutting down

Truffula Trees and keeps "biggering" his factory until there's nothing left at all on the far end of town except some old Grickle-grass. I've heard educators say it's a good way to introduce kids to the value of protecting nature. But in my house, I'm sure that's not the only seed that's getting planted.

A father's time with a daughter is different from that with a son, or a mom's with a daughter, or any other combination. Out of nowhere, I'll hear Alex turn to one of our girls and say, "You're pretty." Or, "You're smart." Or, "You have a kind heart." There is nothing so spectacular or original in these observations, I suppose. A person can likely grow into a healthy adult without hearing them very often, from anyone. But a girl who gets this information, over and over again, from her father? I think he's planting seeds.

Washing dishes to the rhythm of Dr. Seuss can get my imagination working overtime. (Sometimes the bubbles reveal themselves to be elephant-like characters I try to name.) Right now I'm thinking of the seeds, and, in the spirit of things, I imagine them blooming twenty years from now into clanging echoes: "My dad thinks I'm smart. My dad thinks I'm pretty. My dad thinks I'm a good person." You walk around as a grown woman with those messages rattling around in your brain as you brave the world, and you walk around tall, protected, unfettered by the preoccupations of wondering if you're lovable.

Does he know he's doing this? Is he working hard at it, or is this just who he is without thinking? Sometimes I think I'm just getting to know this man, Mr. Popular. The stories he reads at night, his operatic performances, I suppose those are more of the same, more of the messages that say: "You're the most important audience I could ever have."

"Come on, Mom," Anna calls. "*Hurry!*"

Already? It's already time for *moi*? I wipe my hands on a towel and trot with importance into the family room. They're just at the scene with the Super-Axe-Hacker, which whacked off four Truffula Trees with one smacker, and I happen to have a small speaking role.

Ahem.

all pumped up

Zooming into the gas station for a fill-up, I'm feeling smug and sassy. I am so prepared for this, the dawning of multi-tasking season. This year, as the calendar clogs with to-do lists cross-referenced with bus schedules and school lunch menus and work deadlines and football tickets and power-suit shopping and Halloween costume commitments, and all the systematizing of the working mother's life—this year I am *prepared*.

Put it this way: I just got my eyelashes dyed. Yep, I am mascara-free for four weeks, according to Tatiana, the woman who put on the magic gook. With this act, I've just shaved seconds of precious prep time off the docket each morning, not to mention all those glances in mirrors to check for smudges. No more! Not only that, but I've got my calendar computerized. I figured out how to sync my Outlook calendar with my BlackBerry so I can walk around mascara-free and at a glance know where I have to be at any given moment.

In a few moments, I have to be at school to pick up Sasha from preschool. But first I'm filling up my car, because I am a handy two minutes early. This is one of my favorite gas stations because it has the kind of pumps that you can set to automatically fill and shut off—meaning you can leave the pump and multitask. I just multitasked the garbage out of the backseat, and now I'm sitting in the driver's seat checking my BlackBerry.

My in-box shows an e-mail message from my friend Sara, who writes under the subject line "Wee-hoo!" I remember that she went to the outlet mall, where I plan to go this weekend to stock up on school socks and maybe underwear. She is writing with her report of the outlet mall, and with this news: "I just finished my Christmas shopping!!!"

Her what? *She finished her what?* I have to keep rereading the e-mail to fully comprehend the information. But comprehend I do, and as I do I feel my shoulders slump and my neck go wobbly and my head begin to descend into the hell of dismal wretched uselessness.

Christmas shopping? *Chaaaaristmas shopping?* Who has time to even remember Santa, let alone write to him, let alone become him and complete his work? Sara does, apparently, and I realize I must dump her as a friend immediately. But I have more e-mail to read, so I click on it, but now I can't concentrate on anything except Sara and her stupid perfect Christmas, and then out of nowhere I remember I forgot to stop at the store to get those little Tupperware sandwich containers I need because Anna has been complaining about spillage from thermos to bread.

(*Inhale. Exhale. Stay with it, sister. Multitasking season is here and you will survive.*)

I zoom onward toward preschool, cursing Sara and Santa for ruining my mood. I pass a woman flailing her arms. She is jumping up and down near the gas station exit sign, trying to get my attention. Do I know her? Does she need something? I roll down my window.

"The tube!" she is saying. "The, um, the hose!" She is pointing in the direction of my gas tank. Oh. My. God. *And didn't you always wonder if anybody ever did this?* I forgot to take the nozzle out of my car and put it back on the pump. I am driving away with the nozzle and the hose still attached to my car.

"It ripped right out of the pump!" the woman is saying, in awe. "It just ripped right out!"

"Oh, dear . . ." I say, hopping out. "Oh my dear, oh dear . . ." I must have a stricken look upon my eyelash-dyed face, because the woman goes into immediate compassion mode.

"I've got a lot on my mind, too," she assures me. "It's so hard to remember things."

"It's hard to remember not to rip apart the gas pump?" I say.

"Look, the way it came out, I'm sure it was designed that way because people must do this all the time."

"You," I say, "are a good person." I tell her about Christmas. I'm holding the nozzle, dragging the hose back to the pump. She and I agree that, no, I can't just run away and pretend this did not happen.

I lug my wretched self into the little store, wait for the tat-tooed teenager behind the counter to finish talking on the phone, and then I report my crime. "What're you talking about?" she says curtly.

"The hose," I'm saying. "It's off. It's, you know, not on." I find that I don't have the vocabulary for this admission, nor do I seem to have the ability to use the words "I did it."

"Well, can't you just use a different pump?" she says.

"No, I got gas," I say. "But you need to know that the hose, it's *off.*"

"I have no idea what you are talking about," she snarls, fol-lowing me out, and when I show her the damage she gives me the look of disdain and disbelief and horror that I deserve.

Check that off my list. Am I done here? Um. She is still looking, her chin jutting out with expectation.

Me (mumbling): "I don't need to, like, *do* anything, do I? Maybe this is covered under my car insurance . . ."

Her (heavy sigh): "Just . . . go."

I am gone. So far gone.

killing a sheep

If the prolapse is uterine, you must have the sheep's head down in order to put the uterus back in the sheep. If the uterus has swelled, you can put sugar on it to reduce the swelling. It is not always possible to put the uterus back in the sheep.

—DR. BILL REYNOLDS, DVM,
GARDEN STATE SHEEP BREEDERS

We started spatting a lot, Alex and I, ever since lambing season began. Maybe it was birth anxiety, the stress of new life. Just like the pregnant wife who can no longer see her ankles, can hardly sleep what with those little feet stabbing her in the liver—and here's her husband rattling on about how in God's name he'll be able to *handle* changing a dirty diaper. Oh, for heaven's sakes—what in the world is he doing thinking so far into the future while she's sitting there so very locked in the present, a fantastic blob of misery with half a mind to go ahead and explode into tiny shreds if it means getting this creature out of her once and for all?

I've never been pregnant so I am only imagining. Is it anything like being a pregnant farm? We had seven pregnant ewes, one pregnant donkey, a dozen eggs about to hatch, courtesy of our broody bantam silkie hens. A pregnant farm, that's how I imagined myself, and all around me was a landscape teeming with expectation; sometimes I would sit on the porch and believe I could hear the hills swelling, bulging as if ready to burst, *woww, woww, woww*—*hold on folks, here comes a whole new cast of characters.*

A woman *knows*. Any female anywhere near another pregnant female *knows,* and even if she doesn't know she knows, her hormones know. Just like college roommates who find that after a few months their periods are suddenly in sync, women have eerie powers in this arena that we have never figured out how to capitalize on. In my case—and I'm not sure there was any good at all to come of this—I found myself looking at our pregnant ewes, fat as hogs, dragging their massive udders around, and I could completely and consciously and passionately feel their bloat.

(There's a danger, of course, in indulging yourself in this kind of cross-species empathy. Our vet told us that when a donkey is ready to deliver, she'll start "bagging up." That means her breast milk comes in and you can see the swell. So every day I would walk to the barn, bend over, and check, only to be disappointed. Then one day Alex and I were at Applebee's restaurant waiting to be seated at a table for two and the hostess had on a very low-cut blouse and I found myself saying, and way too loud, "Wow, now she's bagging up real good.")

We had, up until that spring, assisted in the birth of just one farm animal: Greg, our goat. So we were in every respect rookies, anxious and excited and testy. Our arguments weren't big blowups, but rather huffy little standoffs. We're by and large respectful. We know how to spit, spat, apologize, and get on with things. Every couple has to learn how to fight. They say parenting either strengthens a marriage or destroys it, and I think mostly it depends on if the two of you know how to manage and forgive each other's incompetence.

I lost the argument over tail docking. Okay, now that was one I didn't even bother pursuing. I thought: Hey, these are his sheep. This is his project. He gets to decide if he wants their tails to be too short.

A day or two after a lamb is born, you're supposed to dock its tail. That means: cut it off. There are several methods of doing this, with preferences seeming to fall regionally. Around us, people use the band method: you put a tight rubber band around the tail, strangling the blood flow, and about a week later the tail falls off. This is said to cause no pain to the lamb, but there could be a lot of wishful thinking supporting that claim.

The reason for docking the tail is not a cosmetic one, as I assumed back in the beginning when I naively proclaimed myself to be morally opposed to the barbaric practice. It was easy to think: Hey, if God didn't want sheep to have tails, He wouldn't have given them tails. A sheep's tail has a function, especially when you are talking ewes; the tail protects the udder from chilling. Docking the tail would seem to be an unnecessary mutilation.

Maybe so, for some Scottish Blackface grazing the rocky Highland hills in search of mere morsels of food. In those extreme conditions, a tail is a good and fine asset, and hardly in the way.

But take your average American Dorset, grazing on our long and lush pastures, and you have a different story altogether, a story you never imagined getting into whenever you first saw sheep grazing on a hillside and fantasized about living a bucolic shepherd's life. Sheep with a lush diet have soft feces. A long tail traps the feces. Flies lay eggs in and around the fecal mass, hatching into maggots. The maggots attack the flesh under the tails, eventually entering the rectum and vagina. A lamb with this condition, known as "fly strike," is a very sick lamb and will almost certainly die.

You just don't need to know a whole lot more about this before you say: "You know what, dock the tail."

Gretta was the first person to introduce me to the fact that there are people in this world who take a *stance* when it comes to where, exactly, to dock a lamb's tail. This was way back when she brought us our ewes, which she purchased for us from a farm in South Carolina. She apologized as the sheep inched timidly off the ramp of the pickup and moved into our awaiting pasture.

"I just had no idea those people docked the tails so short," she said. "This makes me so mad."

"I think they look great," I said, defending the sheep.

"Oh, these tails are way too short," she said, explaining that she had a real issue with farmers who didn't leave at least a little tail length. "Every prolapsed ewe I've ever had was on account of a too-short tail."

I said, "Prolapsed ewe?"

"A ewe that prolapses," she said.

"Prolapse?"

"The vagina falls out," she said.

I looked at her, my eyes all squinted and my head twisting away as I tried to quickly ascertain if, perhaps, it was April Fool's Day and she was working me over.

"Falls out," I said.

"It happens," she said.

"Oh, Gretta, Gretta, Gretta," I said.

She said the reason for the vagina falling out, in her experience, was a too-short tail.

"Oh, Gretta . . ."

"It doesn't happen often," she said, explaining that if it does it's during pregnancy or just after.

"Well, how do you know it's happening?"

"Oh, you *know*," she said.

"How?"

"The vagina falls out," she said.

"What do you mean it falls out? Like, into the body somewhere?"

"I said '*out,*' " she said.

"Like onto the ground?"

"It's a large red mass that hangs from the rear."

"Gretta, Gretta, Gretta."

Standing there watching our sweet yearling ewes sniff and introduce themselves to our ready pasture, I knew right then and there that none of them would ever prolapse. That was something that happened to *other people*, like horrible tornadoes and murders you read about in distant lands.

Even so, I never completely got control of my growing prolapse-anxiety, especially as those ewes went on to become pregnant. It was all part of the mother-empathy engulfing me, as I sat on that porch imagining the sounds of the hills swelling, *woww, woww, woww,* and then feeling all that ewe bloat. On top of all that, or rather below, I was having phantom hemorrhoids. How very terrible. I imagined our ewes prolapsing, and I felt their pain, and what it felt like was a large red mass hanging from the rear, a fantastic, giant hemorrhoid attached to my very self.

"I don't know if I'll survive all this," I said to Alex that day on the porch. "I just wish we would get all this birthing over with."

But he was rattling on, something about grain, about which formula to feed a lamb, and how much, and when—all of which seemed to my bloated self to be quite beside the immediate point.

Our first lamb was born dead. Now, that was really terrible. It was delivered in the middle of the night with no assistance from us, as often happens. But it was dead. I was in the kitchen when Alex came in to tell me, and I went out to see, even though I didn't want to see. When you are in a loving relationship, you show support.

"Well, it's huge!" I cried. And so eerily peaceful. A completely formed lamb, beautiful in its completeness, dead.

"I can't believe this," Alex said. "I just can't believe this."

"Maybe it's the sacrificial lamb," I said. "Like, you just have to get one dead one over with and then all the rest are healthy and perfect."

He didn't answer at first. Finally he said, "It's a bad omen."

"Oh, honey . . ."

"Obviously I did something wrong," he said.

"Oh, honey . . ."

I hate it when he's miserable. I immediately need to undo the misery, like he's got a splinter in his finger and if he would just sit still long enough for me to pop it out, all would be right with him and me and us.

"Hey, wait a second," I said. "Shouldn't this lamb be coated in goo or something? I mean, why is it so clean?" I figured that perhaps lambs came into the world as human babies do, with plenty of mother matter to clean off. Our goat Greg had come into the world this way, and goats and sheep are related.

"The mother probably licked it clean," he said.

We looked over at the ewes, tried to figure out which one had delivered this lamb. None of them looked any different than they had last time we checked, and none of them appeared to be even mildly interested in the dead lamb in the pen.

"Wait a second," I said again, slow and easy like a TV detective who already knew the answer. "Where is the afterbirth?"

We looked around the pen, which was completely enclosed by a fence. We had never seen a sheep's afterbirth, but we figured on at least a small pile of glop. We saw nothing of the sort.

"There has got to be an explanation," I said, and as if to rescue my miserable husband, I went into policewoman mode, pacing slowly around the pen. Then I advanced my theory: this lamb was not delivered by one of our ewes at all. It was . . . dropped here. It was one of George's from just over the hill, and picked up by a hawk, and the hawk was flying and just dropped it right here.

Alex looked at me. "So then why didn't the hawk swoop in and pick it back up?"

"Well, I don't know."

He looked at the sky, as if to actually check for hawk evidence. That was promising. Maybe he was going to buy into this and start forgiving himself, or at least get off the omen theory. Hawks do steal lambs. And we always had plenty of hawks flying around.

"But it just happened to drop in right here in our lamb pen?" he said.

"Hey, things fall out of airplanes and land in swimming pools," I said.

"What?"

"Well, I'm just saying . . ."

He went over to the lamb with a shovel and a shoe box he brought out; his intention was to bury our first dead lamb up under the magic tree, where many of our pets are resting in peace. "It's not going to fit in the shoe box," he said.

"Listen, if you want me to, I'll take care of this," I lied. I was betting he wouldn't take me up on the offer. I can't even walk by the magic tree without howling in pain over Bob, my long-lost cat. Burying the dead has never been my forte. But when you love someone, you throw out offers like this, taking calculated risks.

"I'll do it," Alex said. "You go on inside."

"Yeah, all right," I said, trying not to show my relief.

He came back inside after it was all over, and I put on the TV but he went up to his office and just sat.

A day later our next two lambs were born healthy and strong and it probably was good we had to dock their tails, get busy, forget about that dead lamb. Alex was all Mr. Confidence, holding the little docking tool, sort of like a hole puncher, he picked up out at Agway. I was Ms. Fatigue, feeling the relief of our two ewes who had delivered successfully, my phantom estrogen battling my phantom progesterone and God knows what all else.

I held the lamb while Alex did the docking using the band method. It was hard to know what was too short and what was too long, hard to weigh the risk of fly strike versus that of prolapse. The lamb squirmed as Alex applied the band, and when I put her down she walked like a kid with too-tight pants, but within minutes she was romping as if nothing had ever happened, so we went ahead and docked tail number two.

George stopped over to see our lambs. He had a keen interest, seeing as our ram had been caught over in his field offering its services to perhaps fifty of his ewes, and so our lambs were for him a kind of preview of what his yield might look like. Alex was proud to show George his lambs. Mighty proud of our ram, too, what with all that extra sperm to share. There was so much testosterone swirling amidst the estrogen that spring, it was hard for any of us to see straight. Alex and George stood out there for an hour doing sheep talk.

"Our tails are too long," Alex reported when he came back

in. "George said we have to dock them up higher." He grabbed the tail-docking device and asked if I had time.

"No!" I said. I told him Gretta said they could prolapse if they were cut too short.

"George said they prolapse if the tails are too *long*," he said.

"No, too short," I said, and explained why I thought my way, or rather Gretta's way, made a lot more anatomical sense. "If you cut the tail short you loosen some important muscles up there," I guessed.

Alex shook his head. "Our tails are too long," he said, and he held up the device.

It was one of those standoff moments in a marriage. You have to decide if it's worth it. Soon enough we were in the sheep pen and I was holding the two-day-old lamb while Alex snapped a band about an inch higher than the one we had placed the previous day. I felt disappointed and sorry, but not angry. I figured hey, these are his sheep. This is his project. If it weren't for him and his project, I wouldn't know anything about fly strike or prolapse, anything about how very brutal and gruesome the bucolic life is. It is no more so than regular life, I suppose. There's an awful lot of horrible stuff you have to learn to block out. Any mother who has ever delivered a baby has a lot of cleaning up to do before she can go home and go into coochie-coochie-coo mode in her Pottery Barn Kids nursery with the pastel colors and the super-soft Humpty Dumpty afghan her mother made. It somehow seemed honorable, or maybe elevating, that the lamb, the symbol of peace and tranquility and fabric softener and all good things, had so much going on behind the scenes.

"Sorry about this, girl," I said to the lamb, referring to the inch of tail she was losing, and also to the fact that, like all new parents, we had no idea what in the hell we were doing.

I was in Toronto working on a story when the chicks started hatching, and even though I didn't want any more chickens at all in my life, I was sorry to miss the excitement. Alex called me on my cell phone to tell me about it, and I got hit with the now familiar ache of homesickness. Ever since marriage, and the farm, and the one-two punch of Anna and Sasha, I don't travel nearly as much as I once did. It gets harder and harder to leave, which I guess is a lot better than feeling the opposite.

The story I was researching in Toronto was about a U.S. soldier who had fought for seven months in Iraq, then deserted and fled to Canada. There were six other guys in Toronto I was talking to who had similar stories, and a lawyer who was a Vietnam draft dodger who was helping them try to obtain legal citizenship, but Josh was my favorite and my focus. Before going to Canada, he hid out in Philadelphia for a year and a half with his wife and four children. He was a terrified young man, unsure of his stance on any of this, brittle and naive and soft and hopeful. That's what I liked about him. "Liking" when it comes to writing isn't about liking someone personally, although I did Josh. But this kind of liking is more akin to loving, the way a fiction writer might love a character. You love him for his vulnerability, the tender shell you vow silently to protect even as you imagine exploiting it. He'll give away everything, all of his secrets and all of his pain and all of his heartache if you ask for it. Your job is to listen. Your job is to portray him, in all his glory and all his foolishness, but that doesn't mean you steal his dignity. That's your promise and that's your responsibility.

I loved Josh's tattoos. I loved his wife, Brandi, and her tattoos. She started with the comedy and tragedy theater masks on her back, but she later got that tattoo converted into Gemini panthers above a tulip. I loved that throughout all their troubles, all the rude awakening to an America that once was the land of freedom but became, to them, a land of betrayal—through all of it, they kept a little box they put pennies in, to save for their next tattoos.

These were complicated characters not because of some vast intellect or awe-inspiring talent or spotlight of fame, power, or influence. These were complicated characters because they had been bounced about by the world, thrown this way and that, chewed up and spat out as they tried to make sense of it all. Characters any of us could be.

This was exactly the kind of story I signed up to write, way back in grad school, when I checked the "nonfiction" box instead of "fiction" or "poetry" as my intended genre. Go out and live in the world. Talk to people. Find ordinary people living ordinary lives and start to understand passion and joy and misery in ways you never did before. Re-create those characters on the page. Play with voice, set scenes, stack dialogue, massage metaphors, use all the tools you know how to use to make those characters come alive on the page.

"But *why*?" asked a literature professor who was questioning me a few years ago. I was interviewing to join the faculty of a large English department where I would teach "creative nonfiction," a trendy term that had been invented long after I started writing stories. I hated that term. Why did we even need a term? "Creative nonfiction" made it sound as if we made stuff up, that we were "creative" with our facts, slippery writers taking license with other people's lives. We were not. Worse, it made us sound as if we were begging for respect—that nonfiction writing was somehow and certainly by definition "not creative." Because it deals in facts. Because we begin with the real world as opposed to, as is assumed, the fiction writer's meandering through the imagination, which is somehow presumed to be . . . a more literary place? People never, for instance, have to say "creative fiction" to distinguish it from any other kind. But we have to say "creative nonfiction" to somehow beg for its legitimacy?

Well, if I was a fighter, I would wage a campaign and write long essays for prestigious literary magazines as I gnawed on this stuff. But I'm not a fighter. I don't care enough. I have chickens hatching and kids to get bathed and I have phantom hemorrhoids. If I didn't have all of this, the marriage and the farm and the one-two punch of glory known as Anna and Sasha, maybe I would be a better writer. Maybe I would be a fighter. I would have long days in libraries with nothing more important to do than give my brain daily and huge concentrated doses of literature. I think about this sometimes, and feel regret. I wonder about my deathbed, and regret. I think of God as an army sergeant, giving us life so that we can be all we can be. He gives you a dose of talent, and you're supposed to run with it, and run hard. That's your job. That's why you were put on this earth.

"But *why?*" asked the literature professor who was interviewing me. He wasn't asking about the term "creative nonfiction." He was questioning the whole genre. Why re-create a character from the real world? Why all this playing with voice, setting of scenes, stacking of dialogue, massaging of metaphors, to evoke these characters? Why evoke the characters in the first place?

Well, then. Why do I do what I do? Um. I had been writing nonfiction stories for fifteen years and had never once asked myself why I bothered doing it. What a question! Why does the accountant do what he does? Why do any of us do what we do? Oh my God, we should at least be asking the question! I was sitting there asking myself the question, spiraling into what I figured was my first actual midlife crisis. *How did I end up here? Why did I pick this path instead of some other path? Why do I do what I do?*

I must have had a very contorted upper lip. The room was hot and stuffed with literature professors, all of them leaning back and about to pass judgment, a court of cranky angels you had to pass through before you got through the Pearly Gates. That's what it felt like. A practice round. This was a preview of the afterlife. This was a near-death experience?

But why?

Finally, I shrugged. "I guess you could ask the same question of a photographer," I said. "You know, why take pictures? Or, why does a painter decide to do a portrait of a lady or a man or a dead fox?"

"Dead fox?" one of them said.

Okay, that was stupid. I was thinking of those English hunt pictures you see in fancy homes.

"You do it to evoke emotion?" I guessed. "Or to record history or to have a lasting effect on people?" Or, you do it because you're all worked up about your own mortality? You do it because you have a certain point of view you want to share?

I wasn't sure of any of these answers, which is probably why they came out as questions. "I don't know why anyone creates anything," I said. "It's probably a combination of a lot of things."

Duh. Pull the lever. Send this girl down the chute. No sense even bothering giving God a crack at this one.

I figured the literature professor would come back at me with something, probably something that made use of the word "pedagogy" and maybe "dialectic" and "hegemony" and some of those famous English department words.

But no. He shrugged right along with me. "It's a fun question, isn't it?" he said.

I wanted to kiss him. Oh, so this was a game! This was . . . fun! That was when I realized that reentering academia could be a wild romp as opposed to the slog of drudgery you so often hear about.

I ended up getting the job and loving the romp. It turned out to be an oddly disorienting pursuit to stand in front of a classroom and talk about writing, about researching a story, all the how-to stuff that students have paid good money to learn about. I became a different person in the classroom. A person with lived experience and a bulging brain that was expected to hold wisdom. For the first time in my life I was part of a writing community. How wonderful it was to talk to other people who did what I did! People who went off on stories and gathered facts and came home and stewed over them. I was one of them! I was part of an Us! How very civilized and grown-up! I bought fancy silk trousers and pointy-toed shoes and a briefcase and a new watch and I had . . . appointments.

When I am off on a story, I am not that person. When I am off on a story, I am a kid. I am twenty-six years old, fresh out of grad school, hopping on a barge for two weeks, just letting go of my life, leaving the cat in the charge of the neighbor, while I plod down the Monongahela River with two ornery deckhands and a grumpy pilot and a cook with silver teeth. Sailing off to the ridiculous, not knowing what will happen and gradually entering, becoming a little of them but still a little of me, the me shrinking as they take over. An adventure. That's what I decided my life would be back when I checked the "nonfiction" box. My life would be one adventure after another, sailing off into the unknown, collecting stories and coming home, like a potter who just spent time in a creek bed gathering clay, and making something of my find. An artist. I would be an artist. And so of course I would be lonely. You couldn't form lasting relationships living like that, living like a gypsy. Well, maybe you could. I would have to see. The main thing was art. God gave me a dose of talent; it was my duty to run with it.

And so, walking down Bloor Street in downtown Toronto,

thinking about Josh, thinking about what I needed to say to Brandi, I was excited. I was feeling a familiar kind of alive, being inside a story, tossed about inside an adventure. And then Alex called to tell me the chicks had started hatching, that the girls were jumping for joy, that the girls had actually *watched* one of those chicks peck its way out of that egg, and so naturally I was caught. Caught between this alive and that alive, caught between the life of adventure that by now had become routine, and motherhood, an adventure I had never planned on way back when. But motherhood had come along and when it did it came on like a punch. One-two and three-four and five-six-seven. Punches in my heart that hurt and bruised and demanded to be known, and got that muscle pumping. Motherhood, the mother of all adventures, the great unknown.

I was and remain caught. Caught between a God Who wears army boots and shouts marching orders, and this God, a God in His slippers. "Love," He tells me. "Love comes first, you ninny."

The bright red mass on the back of the ewe looked like a giant ripe tomato. I looked away. I pretended I didn't see it. I pretended it wasn't there. I felt nothing. I felt no hemorrhoids, no bulges, no bloat. Numb. This was weeks after Toronto, weeks after the newly hatched chicks, which were now five yellow balls hopping to and fro, the very picture of spring.

Our "yield" during this, our first lambing season, so far was six. An amazing five females—the more valuable—and one male. He was the prettiest of all, with a coat whiter and smoother than the rest, a kind of kitten. The others were in their own way adorable—you can't look at a gangly lamb with her long legs and tight fuzzy coat and not believe in fairy tales—but the thing that got me was how the five of them all looked exactly the same and none of their mothers seemed the least bit distracted by this. Seconds after a lamb is born it calls, "Meeee," for its mother, and the mother answers, "Meeeeh," and that just seems to do it. The bond is formed; the lamb nurses and the mother licks and it's a real happily-ever-after tale. Occasionally a lamb might get confused and walk up to its aunt for a drink, but that big old girl will nudge her good and send her sailing, so the lamb will cry, "Meee," and the real mother will answer, "Meeeeh," and life goes on.

We had only one ewe that didn't live up to the task. Ironically, it was Sweet Pea, the only ewe with a name, our pet. She had herself been an orphaned lamb; years earlier she had been brought to us by our neighbor George, who thought, perhaps, our nursing goat would adopt her, which she did. I had always held on to that adoption story, a perfect metaphor for Anna and Sasha to think about whenever they got sick of me and wished they had gotten a better mother. "You think you got problems," Sweet Pea could say, "my mother is a goat. . . ."

So naturally I was eager to see what sort of mom Sweet Pea would be. She was the only one of the ewes to give birth to twins, which was in itself heroic, but she rejected one of them. This was not subtle. She threw that baby with one great nudge, flinging it clear across the pen. "Meeee," the lamb said. Sweet Pea offered no reply. She obviously did not consider herself mother to this lamb. Instead she stood and intently licked her second-born, allowing it to drink.

"Meeee," the first lamb said. Again and again, waiting for an answer that never came.

I expected a lot more of Sweet Pea, and felt personally wounded. *After all we did for you?* But I made sure the girls didn't hold her responsible and explained what I learned in one of our sheep books: Birthing can be wildly traumatic for a ewe, especially the first time around. And a ewe with twins has a prolonged labor; sometimes, by the time she finally gets the second lamb out, she forgets all about the first. The pain that triggers the instinct to clean and call and nurture is attached to the thing that came out that stopped the pain. The last lamb. That first one hanging around, waiting for her mother to finish, waiting to get cleaned up and to be fed, might as well be a stray cat or an orangutan. And so the mother nudges it away.

There is always a reason. There is always a logical explanation.

We bottle-fed the lamb and named her Emily.

"Meee!" she would cry.

"Emily!" we would answer.

Sasha, who had just turned four, became the best at this, and made it her job to do those feedings four times a day. I would make up the bottle and warm it for thirty seconds in the microwave and hand it to Sasha, who would walk out back and yell, "Emily!" Those were three pretty distinct syllables for a child with a language disorder to manage, and so at first it came out "Em-we," which frankly we all thought was pretty good.

Changing from "m" to "w" like that in the middle of a word would not have been something Sasha could have accomplished before. But already she had moved far with her ability to speak, defying the odds of the speech therapists who had labeled her apraxic.

Within a few weeks, and with considerable coaching, she was able to say "Em-il-y" as clear as day and we all applauded. She took to running while Emily followed, back and forth along the fence line, Emily leaping for joy at the attention of her mother, and Sasha, like any youngest child, clearly thrilled to have her very own kid to boss around.

All the rest of the sheep stayed with their more traditional mother-daughter sheep pairings and language, "Meee!" and "Meeeeh!"

And so the music filled our fields that spring, the lullabies that inevitably follow the trauma of new life, if everything goes as planned.

Ellen, our babysitter, finally said something about the giant ripe tomato on the back of the one ewe that I refused to acknowledge. "Did you see?" she said. "There's like a big red ball coming out."

"Yeah, I saw," I said. I didn't tell her that I suspected I knew what it was. I just didn't want to talk about it. "Did you tell Alex?" I asked.

"I told him yesterday," she said. "He didn't say anything to you?"

No, he did not. He never mentioned it to me and I never mentioned it to him. If you don't talk about things, they don't exist.

The next day, I went out to look and the tomato was gone. Gone! It seemed to have gone back in. Obviously, this wasn't prolapse. Because it went back in.

"It went back in," I said to Alex. He knew exactly what I was talking about. That was all we said. We were leaving for vacation in a few days. Our first in two years. We were going to Cape May for a week.

Then, the next day, the tomato was back. "The red thing is back," Ellen said. "Did you see it? There's like a million flies on it."

Oh, God.

"It came back out," I said to Alex.

"I know," he said. "I called Dr. Hurley. He said maybe he could stitch it."

When Dr. Hurley came over he said this wasn't vaginal prolapse, but rectal. He said this as if it were a good thing. Congratulations, the vagina wasn't coming out, the rectum was! He said it would likely repair itself.

"We're lucky," I said to Alex. "Don't you sometimes walk around thinking how lucky we are?" Prolapse, the kind Gretta told me about, happens to other people's sheep. We were special. We were not like those other people.

None of the other sheep seemed to take note of the grotesque nature of the tomato, and neither did her lamb, nursing as usual.

Then, the day before we were to leave for vacation, everything fell out. Something broke, perhaps the membrane between the rectum and the vagina, and all the insides of the ewe were spilling out. She was lying on her side, panting, with her baby curled up by her head. The mass of red on the ground was the size of two or three basketballs.

Alex called Dr. Hurley, who said, yes, that must be the membrane. Bad news. He said there was nothing we could do. He said all of her insides, all of the guts, the spleen, the stomach, the intestines, the vagina, the ovaries, all of the things that make a sheep a sheep were falling out. Alex looked at me, shaking his head to say, "Nothing."

"Okay, thanks," Alex was saying and he was about to hang up.

"How are we supposed to do it?" I shouted. "Ask him how!"

"What do you recommend?" Alex said into the phone. "Just, like, a gun?"

Alex listened, looked at me, nodded his head yes.

Ellen came with me outside and helped me pull the baby lamb away from the dying mother. "Meee! Meee!" the lamb screamed. "Meeh," the mom answered. She still had plenty of strength to answer. We took the baby down to the barn and put it into a pen, where she didn't have to watch.

"Meee!" cried the baby.

"Meeeh!" cried the mom.

That was the hardest part. In those cries naturally I heard Anna, and naturally I heard Sasha. I saw someone stealing them from me and them crying for me and me crying for them. But that was ridiculous. That was a silly fantasy. A cartoon. Nothing like that was happening. *Don't be so melodramatic.*

"Meee!" cried the baby.

"Meeeh!" cried the mom.

In those cries I heard Anna and Sasha and the ghost-mothers of China, the loss, the loss, the loss. A torturous image. No sense going there. Nothing you can do about that one. *Now, stop it!*

"Meee!" cried the baby.

"Meeeh!" cried the mom.

In those cries I didn't have to hear or see anything but what was right there in front of me to feel the heartbreak of centuries. A baby losing a mother.

Alex got the pistol. He had fired that thing only once, over on the field on the other side of the road where he had set up a little target practice. I remember because the boom was so loud it sent the dogs running under the bed.

Ellen put on a SpongeBob tape for the girls, hid inside with them.

I told Alex I would go with him, fully expecting that he wouldn't take me up on the offer. He didn't say yes but he didn't say no. He just kept walking and so I followed. The ewe had dragged herself and all of her exposed guts into the large doghouse we had supplied for the lambs, in case of rain. We were surprised she was able to pick all of herself up and move there.

"You think you can just . . . shoot in?" I asked.

"I can't get a clean shot," he said. "I don't know where the bullet would end up."

He grabbed a leg and pulled the sheep out. I didn't offer to help. I should have offered to help. This was all so far out of my league. Wasn't this out of his league? One of us had to step up and I loved him for being the one.

I wanted to say, "Look, if you need me here for this, I'll stay." But I was afraid he might answer in the affirmative. I wanted him to save me. I wanted him to say, "You go on inside."

But he didn't. He wasn't thinking. He was doing. He got the sheep out. She was on her feet, half her insides spilling there. He pointed the gun. I could hear the lamb still screaming. I was so far out of my league. Did he need me to stay? Should I stay? And we didn't say goodbye to the sheep. We didn't thank her and we didn't apologize. Wait!

He wasn't thinking. He was doing. He had the sheep in position, holding her steady by the chest, grabbing her close between his legs. She had no energy to fight. He pointed the gun at the back of her head. Did he need me for this? Should I stay?

I could tell he was going to do it. I could tell there was no turning back. My face was hot and I ran in fear, just took off as fast as I could as I held my hands to my ears as hard as I could and I ran, a chicken, a stupid chickenhearted excuse for a wife. I ran.

The *pow* was more vibration than sound. I felt it through my feet. It was only one shot. I came running inside and I didn't want Ellen to see me cry so I ran to the bed and covered my head with pillows.

"Meee! Meee!" The lamb was out there screaming for her mom, with no reply. None of the aunts filled the void with an answer. None of the goats, nobody. The lamb just kept screaming into the blankness. Say what you will about nature, but nature is cruel and maybe this fact alone helps us forgive our own darkest sins.

It took an hour before Alex came in. He had cleaned everything up. He had taken the body up on the hill, put it in a large pile of brush, and burned it. It was all so very far out of my league.

He looked like hell.

"I'm so sorry," I said, but he didn't seem to hear me.

"I'm sorry!" he said. "I saw you running, I saw you covering your ears." He was close to tears. "You know I never did anything like that before. I never killed anything before. I know you think I'm evil now."

I held him. I told him we were so far out of our league. Gretta would have just gone ahead and made sausage. We had no idea what we were doing, or maybe the problem was we did.

The lamb was still screaming. I told Alex what I heard in that cry, Anna and Sasha and the ghost-mothers. He said he heard himself, still crying for the mom he had lost decades ago. It happens all the time, a child loses a mother. It happens all the time.

We went down to try to calm the lamb down, but nothing we could think of doing worked.

Powerless, we told ourselves we would just have to get used to this. Powerless.

love, kindergarten style

Report from the playground:

The news came from other mothers, from nannies, even from other kids, but not from Anna, who seemed, as is her way, oblivious.

It was big news. Michael had a girlfriend. Anna had a boyfriend. Here it was: Michael and Anna, the first kindergarten couple.

I should have seen the signs. In her backpack each day I would find drawings of green and orange and blue superheroes, some with supersonic goo shooting from their eyeballs. "To Anna from Michael," the pictures would say. Then one day Anna got her first-ever time-out from a teacher. The offense: "Bopping Michael on the head."

Love was in the air. I got the full story from Michael's mother.

"I can't sit next to you anymore," Michael had said to Elaine, the nanny who had devoted her previous five years to his care. "I can only sit next to Anna." It was a major topic of dinner-time conversation in Michael's house. After weeks of hearing about Anna's every move in school, his mother finally said: "What is it about Anna? Is she really nice to you?"

"Oh, she's nice to me," he said. "But she's *so* beautiful."

He announced that Anna was his girlfriend, and that was that. "They're really good together," said one of their class-mates to me one morning by the lockers. Other kids reported on Michael's acts of heroism. When Stevie accidentally knocked Anna over on the playground, Michael ran to her. She was hurt. She was crying. Michael soothed her. "I just petted her and petted her until she felt better," Michael proudly told his mother.

I asked Anna about the incident, and she confirmed the details, adding, "He's a great man."

As the weeks went on, I found myself pushing for news, hoping for bits of intrigue like you do when you read *People* magazine. "So, did anything happen with Michael today?" I would say on the ride home from school.

"No, but Zoe had a hole in her tights," she said once. Much of her news has been of this ilk, and so I've come to depend on Michael's mother and others to keep me apprised.

Inevitably, the crisis occurred: Tritan. He had been Michael's best friend for two entire years. And now Michael was too busy for him. Too busy with a *girl*, of all things. For a while Tritan merely stepped aside, occasionally looking glum. Then he made his move. Michael was handing out invitations to his Halloween party. When he turned to give one to Victoria, Tritan dashed forth. "You can't do that!" he said. "*Because she's mine!*" Victoria was reportedly surprised by the news, but not disappointed. And so Michael found in himself a streak of valor. He did not give the invitation to Victoria but rather handed it to Tritan to give to her. "I *had* to," he later explained. "Because he is my *friend*."

So this, so far, is it: Michael and Anna. Tritan and Victoria. The two happy couples of kindergarten. You can tell that Tritan and Victoria are still in the honeymoon stage, with Victoria only recently getting in trouble for yanking Tritan around by the neck. Michael and Anna have moved on to spats. She got mad at him yesterday; she said he stepped on her foot and would not apologize. He continued to refuse to apologize, despite his mother's insistence in the parking lot after school. "I didn't *do* anything," he said. "And she tried to *kiss* me."

Anna vehemently denies the charges.

It's hard to know where this relationship will go. Last night I overheard Anna talking on the phone to the cousin she hasn't seen since summer. "I have a boyfriend," she announced casually. "His name is Michael. He has black hair, and his pencil box broke."

Tritan and Victoria have already consulted each other on the costumes they plan to wear to Michael's Halloween party. He's going to be "an amazing superhero," and she's going to be "a beautiful Barbie bride."

Anna wants to be a duck.

Michael's mother has expressed her concern. "*A duck?* Are you sure she doesn't want to be Cinderella or something?" She says Michael is having trouble holding in his heart the truth that Anna is actually going to attend this party. *His princess is really coming to his house?*

Yes, and she's going to be a duck.

He's going to be Spider-Man. I have expressed my concern. Anna has been afraid of Spider-Man since she was two. It is as close to a phobia as anything she has. Last summer she noticed a picture of Spider-Man on our Rice Krispies box, and she took the box outside and flung it in the compost pile.

I'm looking forward to going to Michael's Halloween party. An amazing superhero and a beautiful Barbie bride. You can see potential there. But a monster of a Spider-Man and an oblivious duck? I just don't know.

holy days of obligation

Life is a promise; fulfill it.
—MOTHER TERESA

Our ducks were two-day-old ducklings when we got them and somewhere along the line maybe we did something wrong. Maybe that's why they're stupid. All grown up now, nine handsome and rigorous characters, these ducks still can't find our pond. They hang out together in the barnyard, desperately slopping about in any available puddle, the horse trough, a wayward bucket, when just over the bank—about a sixty-second waddle away—is a pond full of lily pads and bugs and cool spring water.

With patience and forgiveness we have escorted them to the pond. We have chased them there and tried to explain. Each time they simply quack neurotically, fitfully, and hightail it back on up to the barnyard.

One hot week I got to feeling sorry for them, so I filled up our little Barbie swimming pool, which they loved. But Alex said I was probably just enabling them so eventually we dumped out the water and went back to chasing them over the bank.

"I'm done worrying about this, ducks!" I shout out my window. "I don't even *care* anymore!" If they want to be dry-land ducks, so be it. I have provided for them a suitable wet-land habitat. I have shown them the way to it. I have done all I can do.

Still, they look so pathetic down there on the driveway, fighting over space in a pothole filled up with rain.

Alex took the girls to the swim club, as a favor to help me get through what is left of this, my rotten day. The idea was to give me some quiet time, some work time, a good three-hour chunk to tend to all the stuff I never got to, on account of the day rotting. It was a kind gesture on his part, it really was, but the fact of the matter is I now feel even worse. All I can do besides worry about the ducks is think of Alex and the girls at the swim club. I think of splashing and frolicking on this sticky night, laughing as the girls play with the plastic blow-up dolphins I won for them last night at the church fair. One of the dolphins is orange and the other is green and I won them by knocking the teeth out of a big, wooden mouth with the little beanbags they gave you, three for a dollar. *Go, Mommy! Yay, Mommy!* I figured out that if you just whacked the mouth hard enough with the beanbag it didn't matter where you hit it because the force would make the whole display jiggle and the teeth would fall out from the vibration. Not once until long after my victory did it occur to me that this technique might be considered cheating (the point of the game was to *aim*), especially there at a church fair where all proceeds more or less go toward salvation. No, I just fired the beanbags, *fwoom, fwoom, fwoom,* and when the teeth fell I jumped victoriously, took the orange dolphin as if it were my God-given right, and then I repeated the whole thing for the green dolphin.

"*Go, Mommy!*" I said, putting the power of suggestion firmly and distinctly right there in the hot summer night air. It's important to sometimes help your children see you as the phenomenon that you are. "*Go, Mommy! Yay, Mommy!*"

The girls did not repeat the mantra, but it hung there, sure it did, like a little tag-along balloon.

Go, Mommy. Yay, Mommy. Have a beer, Mommy. Go soak your stupid head.

Rotten day. This is the way your brain works on rotten days. Little imaginings go from sweet to sour and lead you straight down that spiral staircase of self-loathing.

Last night I had a dream set at Gym Dandy's gymnastics studio, which is where, in real life, Anna and Sasha take tumbling classes on Tuesdays from five-thirty to seven-thirty. Two hours is a long time to stand around a gymnastics studio, let me assure you, but Anna is too old for Roll Tots and Sasha is too young for Kinder Tots, so I had to sign them up for separate classes. In the dream I showed up at Gym Dandy's at the usual time, but it turned out I had forgotten all about the fact that this was the night of the big gym show. All the kids but mine were dressed in their lime green sparkle outfits, ready to perform. "Wait!" I said, insisting that I could be back in twenty minutes with the outfits, if they would be kind enough to afford me one chance to be the hero. I bolted, zoomed home, grabbed the bag with the outfits, but then on the way back I got lost. Around and around in circles I went, as the clock ticked. Then I looked in the seat beside me and noted that the bag I had grabbed did not have green sparkle outfits in it, but rather green *butterfly costumes*. Wrong bag! Wrong outfits! Now I was lost, late, and without sparkle outfits, a perfect trifecta of motherhood malfunction.

I've had dozens of test-anxiety dreams in my life, those nightmares everybody gets when you show up for school having forgotten all about the big exam, or you show up for work having forgotten all about the big presentation. I believe this one to be my first test-anxiety dream: Mom edition.

I couldn't get back to sleep so I put on CNN and soon enough had to try to stop thinking about the fourteen-year-old girl swimming in the Florida panhandle who had just met a most violent death in the teeth of an eight-foot-long bull shark.

Hmm, I thought. Hmm. Then I sang my ABCs, trying to lull myself back to sleep. Then I tried counting backwards from one hundred by threes, which I can never do, so I went by ones, and then the rooster started crowing and so of course the birds started chirping and then I could smell the coffeemaker going, which Alex sets up to start automatically at six.

Whatever. How many recent nights have I spent this way?

How many nights so full of drama and information and failed attempts to go backwards by threes and ABCs and spiraling thoughts of inadequacy? Increasingly the thoughts are not of things I've done to fail my children, but of all the holes. The missed opportunities. The afghan I never knitted when they were tiny. The "life book" I never started in the "scrapbooking" class I never took to learn how to lovingly mount their first lopped locks of baby hair. The photos I never took of them frolicking in fields of daisies with puppy dogs yipping and yapping about. The kites we haven't flown on the sunny beaches filled with laughter and happiness. We've done plenty of these sorts of beautiful things, but not nearly all of the other specifically beautiful things I seem to have on my list; how do you know what is enough and how do you stop yourself from feeling that nothing ever is?

I might be hanging out with the wrong people. If I spent more time with my friends from work instead of my new mom friends, maybe I wouldn't have a to-do list so crammed with fantasies. This morning, after the night of insomnia, I saw my new mom friends and that's when things really went downhill. It wasn't their fault. I love these women. Zoe's mom, Kaitlin's mom, Victoria's mom, and Tritan's mom. These women have their own actual first names, which I have never had the courage to use. I am not entirely sure these women exist outside their roles as mothers; when I am with them I don't either. We have been circling around each other for about three years, ever since our kids started preschool. We'd bump into each other in the parking lot, at Valentine's Day parties, and later as one or the other shyly suggested we all sign our kids up for soft-ball, gymnastics, dance. You do enough of these things together, you bond.

We decided to sign the kids up for a little summer day camp and today was the first day. I trudged up there with Anna with my bleary eyes, the world already feeling all heavy and too much. It turned out that the camp, which was run by the church that runs our school, was a whole lot more Jesus than what I thought it would be. Upon entering, Anna received a "Shape up and ship out with Jesus" T-shirt and then Captain Jesus showed up to take the kids aboard the USS *CHRISTline,* but not before inviting the parents to attend the Captain Jesus Dinner Cruise on Wednesday night at six-thirty featuring Hawaiian Ham Salad and a Surprise Island Dessert.

"Wow," I wanted to say to my new mom friends, and "Whoa." But I didn't know any of them well enough to seek spiritual advice. What sort of religious indoctrination were our children about to receive? Would they undergo exorcisms in the basement? Would they be asked to handle snakes? The charismatic bent was never anything I had run into at school. One of the things I like about having my girls in Catholic school is that I went to Catholic school so I know all the prayers and I've already done plenty of work around doubt, anger, and forgiveness, so I have some sense of how to steer. But I've never been aboard the USS *CHRISTline.* No, I have not.

Zoe's mom had sent Zoe to the camp the year before and had loved it. She was still all gung-ho, so I found myself trust-ing her and kissing Anna and shooing her along inside, then

closing my eyes and just praying, which under the circumstances seemed oddly conflictual.

"So how about we go to Bob Evans for breakfast?" Kaitlin's
mom said, in the parking lot. Everyone said yes to Bob Evans,
except me. I had to work, I said. I had deadlines, I said.

"But you have to eat!" Victoria's mom said.

"I already had my banana," I said, pathetically. I didn't quite
know how to explain that a Bob Evans breakfast would fill me
to the point of needing a nap, as opposed to even a hope of a
good day of writing. Nor did I think my work habits to be of
much interest to anyone, so I said goodbye, drove off, called
Alex on my cell phone.

"Yo, Captain Jesus has invited us on a dinner cruise aboard
the USS *CHRISTline*," I said.

"Whoa," he said. And "Wow."

God bless him.

"What kind of camp is this?" he said.

"I think pretty innocuous," I said, reassuring him that I
didn't think Anna's soul was about to get co-opted by some
loonies. "I'm thinking they just went a little overboard with the
need for a theme."

"All right," he said, generously. His Jewishness and my
Catholicism have coexisted with remarkable peace and tranquility, but the obvious fact is he does the bulk of the compro-
mising.

"All my new friends went to Bob Evans for breakfast," I said,
and I must have sounded forlorn.

"You should go with them," he said.

"You know I can't," I said.

"Yes, you can."

"I have calls to make, a million e-mails before I even get started on my chapter."

"You can take an hour."

"I'll never get anything done if I eat a Bob Evans biscuit," I said.

"You can have a coffee," he said. "And they probably have fruit there."

"Yeah."

I hung up, kept driving toward home, wondering how a person could feel this miserable about not going to Bob Evans, and if anyone else ever did. I was sick of being a working mom. Career shmameer! I wanted to be a regular old mom. I wanted to be a beefy lady choosing the one-stop-shopping convenience at the Super Wal-Mart. A lady with three screeching kids tugging at her shorts and a baby in the shopping cart and a case of Slim-Fast underneath that she would swear she would drink instead of any more of those damn SpaghettiOs.

Those kinds of moms, I thought, now those are the kinds of moms who knit afghans and make life books and mount locks of baby hair. Why am I answering the call of a nagging, stupid career, instead of just being one of those kinds of moms?

Worse—I am trying to do both. Like so many women, I am trying to do both. How ridiculous. What a perfect setup for failure.

Too damn much. Work plus motherhood, the weight of conflicting responsibility on top of responsibility. Driving home, still half-drunk from my night of insomnia, I wondered if my problems sleeping weren't just this. Nothing so spectacular. Responsibility piled onto responsibility. Just too damn much.

The kids. The farm. A weekly column to write, a monthly column to write, three feature stories to write, a book to write. Teaching. My garden, such as it is. The goats need to be wormed. Skippy's hooves need to be trimmed. E-mail. Old friends and new mom friends. Calling my mother. A birthday card for my sister. A dentist appointment. Helping Sasha learn how to talk. Standing by the pool applauding because Anna finally got the courage to put her face in the water.

Nothing so spectacular. Nothing heroic or memorable or even honorable. Just too damn much.

Any working parent, or, for that matter, any parent, goes through days with the circus plate-spinner image in her head. Getting everybody fed, and Jimmy to soccer practice, and Betsy to ballet class, and little Junior out of his stinky diaper— all at the same time—conjures up the notion of the classic circus performer. Implicit in the metaphor, of course, is a certain admiration for the person who can stand in front of a crowd in a flashy outfit and get even one plate spinning on the end of a long pole, let alone two, three, four, five, six, seven, and eight. Watching something like that is sure to trigger awe. But sooner or later, certainly when the guy gets up to ten, twelve, maybe fifteen plates spinning on the end of long poles, and he's dashing madly about to keep each one a-spin, you might look at him and think: But *why?* You know, what is the point of this exercise? Has mastery of this particular skill set advanced the course of humankind?

Responsibility. The circus performer has accepted responsibility for each spinning plate, and so that's what we watch and that's what we admire. Accepting responsibility is good, is righteous, is noble. Anyone will tell you that.

"The price of greatness is responsibility," Winston Churchill said.

"Knowing is not enough; we must apply," Goethe said. "Willing is not enough; we must do."

"Do more than is required of you," George Patton said.

The history of the universe is littered with people making inspirational and enduring statements about taking, accepting, and celebrating personal, moral, political, and social responsibility.

So, go, Plate Spinner, go! I should celebrate my plate-spinning pursuits, not duck them, and for pity's sake not whine about them. I should be proud. I should come up with an inspirational and enduring quote.

Oh my God, one more thing to do. One more plate. *Is someone throwing plates? Is this a dirty trick? A practical joke?*

Now, *shirk* is a good word. Can you shirk anything besides responsibility? You have to admit it's impressive to have a word, *responsibility*, so powerful as to have its own dedicated word to describe the act of defying it. Shirking responsibility should have been on those tablets Moses came down with, or maybe the point was too obvious. Everyone knows shirking responsibility is wrong; God didn't even need to remind us of that one.

Shirk. To shirk. Shirking. What a delicious word to play

with and roll around your tongue. Oh, I could taste it. I could smell it.

It smelled like Bob Evans biscuits. Yes, it did. And Bob Evans was where, I decided, I was bound.

I pulled into the Sunoco, turned around.

Liberation! I was a drunk going for a drink. I was a straight-A student skipping the whole stupid exam and refusing to care about this, her first F.

Wee-hoo! Bring on the biscuits.

Playing a little hooky now and again is good for the mind, of course it is, good for the heart and good for the soul clogged with sins. Drano for the soul. *Mr. Plumber!* Oh, I was long overdue.

I remembered Kaitlin's mom saying something to Tritan's mom about going to the Bob Evans on Route 18, but I might have heard that wrong. I knew of only one Bob Evans, and it was just off Route 19. So first I looked on 18, then got lost trying to take a shortcut over to 19, thinking how stupid it is to have a Route 18 and a Route 19 in the same town, 18, 19, 19, 18, I wondered if Bob Evans had oatmeal. Blueberries? On 19, I got stuck behind a truck carrying half a mobile home that had the whole road blocked up. I wanted to cry. I wanted biscuits. I never wanted biscuits so bad.

I found Bob Evans but not my new friends. They had either already left or else there was another Bob Evans somewhere I didn't know about.

I drove home. "I'm worthless," I told Alex. "I can't handle responsibility and here I'm no good at shirking it either," I said. I was an alcoholic who decided to fall off the wagon—only to find all the liquor stores closed. At a time like that you don't feel saved from yourself. No, you do not. You feel cheated.

"Rotten day," I said. "I am having a rotten day."

Okay, so now the ducks have moved from the pothole to an unopened package of Owens Corning forty-year roofing shingles. The wrapper on the package is bubble gum pink. The ducks are eating it. All nine ducks, just tearing away at that package with that spastic nibbling action ducks are famous for.

This can't be good. What is the matter with those ducks?

I swear to God they're playing with me. "*If you don't fill up our Barbie swimming pool we're just going to stand here and eat plastic!*"

Eventually, I give in and get the hose. When Alex and the girls get home, I'm standing by the Barbie pool watching the ducks splish and splash, holding the hose.

"I thought we weren't going to let them use the Barbie pool," Alex says.

"I couldn't take it anymore," I say. "I have a responsibility to these damn ducks."

"Yeah, but—"

"They were eating the roofing shingle package."

"Yeah—"

"I'm taking care of the damn ducks. Because this is my response-a-bila-tee. Do you understand?"

"Are you okay?"

"I have re-sponse-a-bila-tees," I say.

"You have a creepy look in your eyes."

"Re-sponse-a-bila-tees! Tra la la!"

"Sweetie, are you okay?"

"Ma! Up! Up!" I hear, as if through a tunnel. It's Sasha, standing right here at my hip, her arms up in that pleading way she has. I sigh. One more thing is going to put me over the edge.

"Up! Up!"

One more thing.

"Up!"

What, I don't want to pick up my own kid? It's *too much?*

She's all shriveled and waterlogged in her bathing suit, and I can't take one more thing, not even this tiny little thing, but no matter. I am her mother. I am called to duty. I scoop her up. She smells like a chlorine bomb. I balance her on my hip and the smell of her and the feel of her next to me, making my shorts soggy, is a rescue.

The exhale coming out of me seems to fill the valley.

"Sweetie," I say. "Aw, sweetie. Did you have fun at the pool?"

"Yes." She puts her cheek next to mine, squeezes.

"Aw, sweetie."

My God, motherhood is a rescue. It just is.

"Come on, girls, let's go inside," I say.

"You okay?" Alex says.

"I'm okay," I say, handing him the hose. "How about you finish the duck bath and I'll do the kid bath."

"I'm turning off the hose," he says. "I am turning it off."

I take the girls in. I check their heads for ticks. I peel their bathing suits off and start the bath and offer bubbles and little cups and plastic frogs. They want it all. I sit next to the tub. I always sit right here on the floor next to the tub, in case either of them should go down and I have to immediately yank them out. This has never happened, not even close, but you hear stories.

I like it on the floor. I have magazines here. I root through the stack and can't find one *Newsweek* I haven't already read. What, we don't get any magazines besides *Newsweek*? I pick up one of Alex's psychological journals and flip through. In the bath, Anna says her frog is a Kitty Frog and proclaims that Sasha's is a Princess Frog and so their story begins. Bubbles are castles, cars, horses. The Kitty Frog does what the Princess Frog tells her to, until the Kitty Frog decides to spit and burp and then it gets gas. The Princess Frog thinks this is hilarious and gets gas, too.

"All right, girls," I warn, "this is getting gross."

I turn to Alex's journal and read. I read about a woman at Université Laval in Quebec, sitting in a room sorting capsules. Fifty capsules. Her job is to put them in bottles according to color. She does this, then hands her work in to the researcher in charge of the inane task. The researcher then explains the purpose of the exercise. He tells her that he specializes in the perception of color and that he has been mandated by a pharmaceutical company to undertake a widespread project concerning the exportation of a medication for a virus spreading in Southeast Asia. The region is very poor and its population uneducated, so they need to develop a system of colors that will make the distribution of medication fast and accurate.

"Hmm," I say to the girls. "Hmm."

"Kitty Frog has a terrible bellyache, Mommy," Anna says. "She just has the worst gas."

"Princess Frog has di-a-reee-ah!" Sasha says, believing herself to have found the funniest line of the day.

The girls howl and I go back to the capsule sorter, who tries again after getting the point—her ability to sort the colors correctly will directly influence the manufacturing of the medication.

So she sorts again, and naturally she's more careful the second time around. Forty other women and ten men are asked to perform the same series of tasks, first without the knowledge of the drug's purpose, and then with it. Some of these people have been pre-identified as scoring very high on a scale of perfectionism, the rest average.

Only after they are finished with the second round of sorting do the subjects learn the rest of the story: this was all a sham. There is no widespread virus, no poor population, no drug, no pharmaceutical company. In actual fact, the experiment was intended to test a burgeoning theory among researchers seeking to understand obsessive-compulsive disorder. Was "an excessive sense of responsibility" at its core?

"Hmm," I say to the girls. "Hmm."

The Princess Frog has started to attack the Kitty Frog and water is everywhere so I pull the plug and the girls get out of the tub. I wrap towels around them and then I rake a brush through Anna's knotty hair and then I recheck both of them for ticks. Anna has a freckle on her scalp that looks exactly like a tick and I can never seem to completely convince myself that it isn't one.

I have an excessive sense of responsibility, I think. Or just excessive responsibilities? How can you tell which? Apparently, if I'm guilty of the former, I'm screwed up. An excessive sense of responsibility, I read, is at the root of obsessive-compulsive disorder. "Checking behavior" is one of those buzz terms they use when they talk about OCD. People with "high incidences of checking behavior" are said to have the disorder. There's a line. Normal people sometimes need to double-check themselves. OCD people have to quintuple-check, over and over again.

An excessive sense of responsibility is said to be at the root of this. And what it comes down to is this: you think you're more important than you are. You think your actions *matter* more than they actually do. Despite what you believe, you are just not that *critical* to keeping the earth spinning on its axis.

I know I'm not. I know! I kick the journal across the bathroom floor, so as to rescue myself, and this rotten day, which appears to be officially decomposing.

The girls are exhausted and give me little trouble going to bed. Anna stacks her four special pillows just so, with her designated Guardian Angel pillow right there next to her head, and the ice bag she has come to like on top of her head, and the little glasses of ice chips surrounding her. It's . . . complicated. It's a ritual. She has moved in and out of a million crazy bedtime rituals, and daytime rituals, too, now that I think about it.

"Angel of God, my guardian dear," she begins, then, "To whom God's love commits me here, ever this day be at my side to light to rule to guide—*no dreams for Anna until she's a grown-up and Sasha would like good dreams only*—amen."

Anna thinks of herself as a general in the war against bad dreams. She has it worked out that guardian angels are the soldiers doing the dirty work (if they see a bad one coming, they'll kick it into the sky where it will dissipate, like some exploding asteroid) and if she says the prayer, with that little extra line thrown in, she won't get any bad dreams because her guardian angel will have thus been dispatched. To give herself extra protection, she cancels out *all* dreams, not just the bad ones for herself, and she would do this for Sasha if she requested it, but so far Sasha has not. This system, apparently, works quite effectively.

"Good night, girls," I say, wondering if I should curtail this child's imagination. Should I start her now understanding that she is not central to the universe spinning on any particular axis?

God, I have so much to do.

"I love you, too," Anna says. She never waits for me to say it first, but rather for the send-off line she has come to depend on:

"That makes me happy," I say.

"I luff woo, Mommy," Sasha says.

"I love you girls a thousand million trillion percent," I say.

"I love you infinity," Anna says.

"I luff woo more!"

"All right, girls."

Alex is in bed eating ice cream, a huge bowl of it atop a piece of chocolate cake, finished with whipped cream and a cherry he is saving. He's watching *Law & Order*. Mr. Relaxation. Mr.

Not-a-Care-in-the-World. I want to be him. I want to . . . get there.

"I don't think I have excessive compulsive disorder," I announce.

"Oh?"

"There's a link between OCD and an excessive sense of responsibility," I say. "But I don't think I have that, either."

"No," he agrees.

"I just have a lot of responsibilities," I say. "Any mother does. Anyone who takes the job seriously. And then when you throw work on top of it, it's . . . a lot."

"Of course."

"But it does not mean I have excessive compulsive disorder."

"No," he says. "If you did have obsessive-compulsive disorder, you wouldn't be calling it 'excessive compulsive disorder.' "

I look at him. "Is that what I said? 'Excessive compulsive disorder'?"

"About sixteen times," he says.

Oh. "Well, that's good news then, isn't it?"

"I think so."

I climb into bed. We stare at the TV. He eats his ice cream. I close my eyes and begin a list of all the things I am not going to worry about if and when I awake at 4 a.m., as per usual, which I know is a recipe for insomnia and so I yank myself free. I start counting backwards by threes, get stuck at seventy-two. I say my ABCs. Nothing is working. I try Anna's guardian angel prayer, slightly edited. *No dreams for Mommy until she's, um, dead, amen.*

I drop like a bomb into sleep. I do not have any dreams. In

the morning I awake, stretch, look out the window, and prepare myself for another day of forgiving the ducks. Where are the ducks? Every morning they're usually right here, outside the bedroom window, pecking through the geraniums for bugs. Why aren't they here? I throw my sandals on and head down to the pond to see if perhaps God has taken care of this job overnight; the sight of nine gleefully splashing ducks would certainly fit my mood on this post-perfect-sleeper morning. "Hallelujah, ducks!" I will say.

But no. I find them leaping into the air, one, two, three, taking turns trying to access a puddle formed at the bottom of the girls' tire swing.

"This, ducks, is getting embarrassing."

So, Zoe's mom just called to say Zoe is expressing some confusion about Captain Jesus. We have just completed day three of camp.

"Mom, I thought Jesus was dead," Zoe reportedly said. "The nails through the hands? The cross?"

"Well, He did die, honey, but you know that's not the end of the story." She started to remind Zoe of Easter.

"So He came back as a captain? He drives a boat?"

"No, honey. That's not the real Jesus."

"Yes it is, Mom. He is real. I saw Him."

"No, sweetie, that one's more like a mascot. Like, at Disney World?"

This explanation apparently did not help Zoe sort through her spiritual crisis.

I tell Zoe's mom that it's probably very good Zoe is articulating her confusion about Jesus returning to earth as a nautical figure. I tell her Anna has yet to even mention the captain, although at night she has been walking around our house in song:

"Love one anudder. Love one anudder. Love one anudder . . . as I have loved you."

She was already on to the second verse before I had a chance to correct her:

"Care for each udder . . ."

I was so afraid of the possibility of finding out that Anna thought this was a song about cows that I decided to just let it go.

She is such an unaware child. Academically, she is rungs ahead of her classmates, but ask her what she had for lunch and she will look at you blankly. She will, no doubt, grow up to be a book-smart person with little common sense and dressed, now and again, as a kitty. She has been dressing as a kitty on and off since she was two, a headband of fuzzy ears, feather boa wrapped around her waist to simulate a tail, and whiskers painted on.

"Face it, she's eccentric," my sister Claire recently said. This when she got wind of the fact that Anna had started sleeping with the ice bag on her head, and the ice chips on her nightstand. She just wanted to sleep . . . surrounded by ice.

"Whew," Claire said. "Eccentric."

"And your point is?"

"I just want to understand her mind—"

I suppose I could try to curtail Anna's odd behaviors, try to
rein her in, but why? What good would it do? She's a happy
kid. She's well behaved. She does well in school and has begun
to form friendships. Sometimes I imagine her having been
adopted by another mother, someone with little patience for
neurotic behavior, someone who would try to *reason* with her
and I think, *Whew.* She landed in the right place.

If I have one overarching responsibility to her and her sister,
I suppose it is in applauding them as they grow, unhindered,
into the people they are aching to be.

It isn't until day four of camp that Anna finally comes home
with a Jesus observation. "Mom, Jesus goes to camp," she says.

"Oh?"

"Yeah, He comes off a boat," she says. "But not a real one.
It's, like, cardboard."

"Oh."

"But Jesus is real, right?"

"Well, of course Jesus is real, but—" I don't quite know how
to field this one, and I wonder if perhaps she and Zoe have
been sharing spiritual doubts. I'm so happy she's asking. I'm so
happy for this opportunity. What is a mother's number one job
if not to guide her child through life's mysteries? "I mean, Jesus
is always with us," I say.

"Well, He sure knows a lot of songs," she says. "He has a
good voice."

"That's . . . good."

"Then He goes behind a curtain, but I don't know what happens to Him back there."

"Oh, I'm sure He's fine back there," I say.

"Oh, I'm sure He's fine," she says. "He probably gets a hamburger. Plus He has to feed His cats."

"Jesus has cats?"

She shrugs.

"Did they teach you today that Jesus has cats?" What the hell kind of camp is this?

"No," she says. "I don't know how I know that. Sometimes you just know things, Mommy."

"Right."

In Anna's mind, all is fine with Jesus, so I don't see any point in pushing it. But then again I sort of do. I stand here with my lips pushed out and my eyeballs stuck up in the ten o'clock position, the very portrait of competence.

In a happy turn of events, a few days later the ducks find the pond. They're down there swimming hysterically, gleefully bobbing their heads in and out, and so we all go down to watch. It is one of God's minor works, I know, but these days I am clinging to any miracle I can get.

the young folks' home

"Inside every old person is a young person trying to get out." This is my mother's maxim for the weekend. She often has one of these sayings she walks around with. I'm certain she makes them up, but her authoritative delivery has a way of suggesting Aristotle or Benjamin Franklin.

The new saying has been her refrain as she watches her granddaughters, with their infinite energy. She keeps catching herself. She thinks, for a split second, that she can jump out onto the driveway and join them on their tricycles, and then, in a burst of awareness, she remembers.

"Inside every old person—" she says.

"I know, Mom," I say. "You already told me."

This is the first time in about four years that my parents have visited our house. It is, in that way, a big deal. All their previous attempts over these past years were thwarted by illness—a broken hip, a heart thing, an intestine thing, a whole bunch of undiagnosed things, neuropathy. "Face it," my mom told me last summer, "we're too old."

Her surrender only made me more determined to help my parents make the five-hour trek to my house. Recently I cooked up a deal with my brother, who would drive them out. When it finally looked like it was really going to happen, I got on to the business of worrying. Would they be comfortable here? We live on a slope. We have a lot of mud. We're hardly handicapped-accessible. Would they be able to handle the noise of my rambunctious girls? And all the stinky pets?

So I reserved a room for them at a nearby hotel. One of those suite places with a walk-in shower and no steps. I washed the dogs. I told my girls, "Now listen, they're *old*, so you can't be bashing into them."

"They could fall over?" Anna asked.

"They could fall over," I said.

"Well, I would like to find out how they got so old," she said.

My parents took on celebrity status as we prepared for the visit. Actual old people *in our house*! We see plenty of senior citizens when we visit my parents in their retirement village, but this would be the first time my girls had them on the home turf. I didn't think the novelty factor would last. In fact, I worried that my kids would quickly grow bored with the old folks, as kids do. I figured my job for the weekend would be to keep the old folks entertained, while at the same time keeping the kids . . . quiet.

And now look. We're already on day three of the visit, and

the novelty has not worn off. At the moment, the two old people and the two young people are hunkered down together in my living room. It's raining outside. My mom is on the couch drawing pictures of cats and witches and rainbows with Anna. On the big leather chair next to them, my dad is all smiles and applause, as he watches Sasha dance and bow and curtsy.

I'm watching this. I'm thinking: Well, this isn't a disaster at all. I'm marveling at just how well old people fit with very young people, and vice versa.

Sasha is all flirt. My father is all flirt. These two have discovered each other in a way they never have been able to before, when we're at the retirement village and all the cousins are around. Sasha has been following my dad, curling up next to him and, in her Sasha-speak, whispering in his ear. "Bess frenz, Granddat," she said this morning. "Bess frenz."

Anna, the artsy sister, has taken charge of my mother, an artist who had her muse largely stolen by a body of aches and pains. My mom has not drawn this much in years. She has found in Anna a mission: "You're going to be an artist when you grow up, aren't you, sweetie?"

Anna looks at her with gentle confusion. "I *am* an artist," she says.

The two have been working all day on a picture book about how people get old. Anna thinks her hair will get curly like Grandmom's and that she'll walk on very skinny legs.

It has gone on like this, these four people, two old, two young, forming a club that excludes the likes of me. I'm the cooker and the cleaner and the driver. I wonder if I've ever been so happily irrelevant.

When the rain stops, Sasha is the first to react. She grabs her shoes, then finds my father's shoes. She wants to take him out to the sliding board. He says, well, then, let's go get a towel and dry that sliding board off! My mother protests. She says he won't be able to climb the hill to the swing set. My father says, yes, he will. My mother says, well, then, he has to take her cane. The negotiations continue. Eventually, I stand with my mother at the kitchen window and we watch my father out there splashing in puddles.

"Inside every old person is a young person trying to get out," she says.

Yeah, well, I guess he made it.

the foggiest notion

In the beginning there was fog. That's how that one should have started. Every new idea, the dawning of every adventure, begins in the worst kind of fog—thick, murky slop you can't see through and so you half consider pulling over and going to sleep.

Alex is plugging along. He's just chattering away up there, leaning forward as if that will help with visibility, telling stories about the good old days in college, and quoting Voltaire.

We're in the pickup. It's after 2 a.m. We are somewhere in the mountains of West Virginia, driving home, and I'm squished back here in the so-called "extended cab" portion of the truck, Anna snoring on my left shoulder and Sasha's head, hot with dreams, resting on my thigh.

Behind us we're towing a horse trailer and inside the horse trailer we have "À Votre Santé," an enormous four-year-old

Standardbred gelding, and "Strong Fort," an even more enormous ten-year-old Thoroughbred gelding. Both of these big boys, with a combined weight of well over three thousand pounds, are retired racehorses, and we are taking them home to live with us.

I can't believe we're doing this. I can't believe no one in this truck is saying, "I can't believe we're doing this." Even I think we're lunatics, and I'm usually the one cooking up schemes like this, owing in part to my failure to fully tame my inner Lucy Ricardo and my inner Ethel Mertz.

But this, yes, this is bigger than Lucy and Ethel. In this darkness and in this fog, I am officially cowered.

Up front next to Alex is Cindy, our new friend who used to be our dog groomer but then evolved into our horse trainer/instructor. Next to Cindy is her boyfriend, Bob, who used to work as a trash collector but last year he fell off the back of the trash truck going at an illegally high speed, so he quit trash collecting and started college instead.

So, we're driving. Alex has remarked more than once that he can't see five feet in front of him. He is wisely going just thirty-five miles an hour on this highway. His point is that if we have to stop suddenly, the tonnage of horse meat behind us is sure to create some drag. Fortunately, no one else is on the road. We've passed a lot of rigs parked over in rest areas, apparently preferring the aforementioned option of snoozing. Every time he sees one of those idle rigs, Alex points it out. I can tell it's because he thinks he's heroic, pushing on while even the pros have surrendered, and that he wants acknowledgment.

"You're amazing," I say, because this is what a spouse should say. And because I have to admit I'm impressed. I would never drive in this stuff, with or without the baggage. I could not do this alone. That's what's impressing me. The common conclusion is always that I'm the one responsible for creating this family, that it's all my inner Lucy and Ethel fueling us to get a farm, adopt kids, go chicken and duck and sheep and goat and horse shopping. But look, folks, look who's driving. If it were up to just me, none of this family would have happened at all. I wish I knew how to give him more credit, and if he wants it.

We've got about ninety miles to go. Besides giving Alex credit, all I can think about is how big those horses are. It's the bigness that is getting to me.

"You know what?" Alex says. "I'm starting to think I'll be able to see better in this fog if I just turn these headlights off."

"Oh, honey, I don't think so . . ."

"Oh, no!"

"Oh, dear . . ."

"What happened?"

No, we most definitely can't see better without light. Now we are towing our bigness down this highway in the pitch and total dark. We are a misguided missile falling off a plane; we are an asteroid dropping through space; this is the beginning of something new or this is the end of everything. This is it. We'll crash here. In the morning they'll be talking about the traffic delays on I-79. They'll be talking about the tragedy, six people, two of them children, and two horses splashed all over the highway, such a shame. Traffic on I-79 northbound will be backed up for miles while they clean up the mess, so please, folks, find an alternative route.

"Okay, that's better," Alex is saying, finding the switch and turning the lights back on.

Here, as our summer has begun to slip toward fall, here we are with a whole new horse life. It seems to have come out of nowhere, but if I look back I can see the pieces falling together over the years, little pixels arranging themselves haphazardly, and then suddenly the picture begins to emerge.

Did we even want a horse life? Was this ever even an objective? In the spring we signed the girls up for horseback-riding lessons at a local stable with the idea that if they're going to grow up on a farm they should know how to behave around horses. It was a safety issue, on the one hand, and an experiment more or less on behalf of our three beloved equines on the other. Alex and I had long since stopped paying attention to Skippy, my mule, and Maggie, his mare with the sore feet, and even Blitz, the pony I naively got for the girls when they were still way too young.

Yes, I suppose we did want a horse life, that much is obvious, and I can see that over the years we flirted with the idea as we tried to manage the difference between fantasy and reality. Fantasy is you and your husband blissfully romping over the hillsides atop your big, strong stallions, and wearing your cute little riding hat and those slick tight pants and boots, don't forget the boots! And who's that emerging from the bushes? Oh, hi, sweeties! It's your little girls on their fine ponies, one wearing braids and the other with her rosy cheeks, *clip clop, clip clop,* come on, family, let's gallop together toward the top of the hill where our *tea party awaits!*

Most dreams start out as cartoons. If you knew about all the work, all the financial as well as emotional outlay involved with the dream, you'd never talk yourself into bothering with it.

Skippy and Maggie came into our lives long before the girls. That's when the fantasy was still in the Mr. and Mrs. stage, no kids in the picture. I fell in love with Skippy and I encouraged Alex to fall in love with Maggie and we tried to figure out which end of our new saddles pointed forward and what, exactly, a bridle was. We didn't know how to tie a cinch knot, let alone how to ride. We took some lessons. Alex even built a round pen on the other side of the road where we would go and practice, much to the amusement of Skippy and Maggie, both of whom had our numbers. (*"These people are idiots."*)

When you are new at riding, the first thing that hits you is that the very large animal beneath you doesn't want to do what you want it to. No, that large animal would really prefer to go back to the barn and eat. This may be fine for bossy types determined to conquer beasts, but for regular old animal-lovers who come from a basic dog-lover culture, it presents challenges. Dogs want to please you. Dogs will do anything for a scratch behind the ears. Dogs are smaller than you and depend on you.

Horses are . . . big. Horses outweigh you by about half a ton and so they really don't have to pay any attention to you if they choose not to. And why would they choose to? That's what I could never get. Who was I to boss Skippy around? Skippy had been trained by a famous mule trainer, had won ribbons in rodeos, so I knew he wasn't the problem. It was me. I was not worthy. I was puny and unentitled. "Oh, I'm sorry!" I would say to him when he wouldn't obey my most tentative commands.

"Aw, sweetie, you don't want to go around the ring today? I'm sorry. Poor baby. Mama's gonna take you home and give you some treats. . . ."

As I tried to learn to ride Skippy, mostly what I did was turn him into a spoiled brat. It got so that mule would do nothing that I asked of him. Why would he?

Alex was better at handling Maggie, who was, however, clearly too small a horse for him. Her thin back was no match for his manly thighs and every time he'd mount her you could see her eyes pop out in pain.

Alex fell off Maggie and broke a rib during this period, and Maggie's feet developed problems so then she really couldn't handle his weight, and then Anna came, and then Sasha. One thing I learned is you can't do motherhood and horseback riding at the same time. At least not early motherhood. These two lives have virtually zero intersection. One could conceivably strap one's child papoose-style on one's back and ride one's mule, but one such as me would probably and rightfully be hauled off to the Department of Children and Family Services.

So Skippy and Maggie went on about their lives in the field, occasionally getting called in for carrots. We loved watching them graze up on the hill with the backdrop of the setting sun. We got insulted when Mike, our farrier, would come to trim their feet and call them "expensive lawn ornaments."

Hey, we took good care of them. What was wrong with having equines as pets? We got Blitz when Anna was four and Sasha was two because a friend was selling him and I knew he was a bomb-proof pony, and I was watching *Mary Poppins* a lot, feeling inspired by that scene when Julie Andrews and Dick

Van Dyke go sailing with the kids on those carousel horses that magically prance about the colorful English countryside.

The farrier was the one who told us about Storybrook Stables and the group lessons for kids. He said it might be good to teach our girls to ride on horses that have been kid-tested, and then maybe, someday when the girls were older, we could rescue our equines from their lazy days of munching toward equine obesity.

At first, the main reason Anna wanted to take horseback-riding lessons was because Michael, her boyfriend, had agreed to take them with her. She was six now and she and Michael had been an item since they were both five, when they met in gymnastics class. That's where the sparks first flew. So much of Anna's little life changed in that gymnastics class. It was supposed to be Sasha's thing. I thought Sasha's tiny little body would be a natural at tumbling, and some of her speech therapists had said that the lessons in movement and coordination and muscle-sequencing would ultimately help her speech.

I figured Anna would drop out of gymnastics after a few weeks, preferring something more cerebral. Delayed physically in so many ways when we adopted her—at eleven months she couldn't even sit up or roll over on her own—I never figured on her being much of an athlete. She was always "the artsy one." And Sasha was "the spitfire," "the flirt," the girl who would try anything once.

Labeling children one way or another is something all parents say they'll never do and lo and behold all parents do.

But Anna blossomed in gymnastics. Soon she could do a perfect cartwheel and in no time a round-off. She was becoming known for her athleticism. Her *athleticism*? It took a while for this to sink in. And the athleticism had brought her out of her shell, out of the AnnaLand she had so blissfully lived in before; now, so comfortable in her body, in the physical world, she was ready to come out and play.

But it was in the horse life that Anna found a real home. Soon, at riding lessons, the instructors came out to watch the six-year-old who possessed the posture and poise and confidence of an experienced rider. She was a natural, they all said. It seemed as if when she was on that horse she was once again in AnnaLand, fully focused in the moment, in the intersection of muscle and mind, and somehow she found a way of allowing the horse to be right there in AnnaLand with her.

She would come home and draw pictures of all the ponies at Storybrook Stables, and tape them to the wall. She had me look up the difference between an Arabian and a Quarterhorse and a Palomino and other breeds, information she memorized until she could recite it on command. Horses were becoming her everything.

She was on the porch drawing horse pictures the day Cindy came over to groom Marley. Cindy was standing there freeing Marley's poodle curls of burrs, and I was going on and on like a proud mother does, bragging about Anna and Sasha and their natural skills at riding at Storybrook Stables. Sasha was too small to have quite the strength and prowess of Anna, but her daredevil spirit allowed her to keep up with Anna if only in that she did not mind falling off anything. A bloody nose here and there, a scraped elbow. No big deal. She would climb right back on.

Cindy asked the obvious question: We had horses. We had fifty acres of fields and woods upon which the horses could ride. Why weren't our daughters riding our horses?

"*Our* horses?" I said. "Oh, we would never trust them on our horses."

"What's wrong with your horses?" she asked.

"They're sweet," I said. "But they're wild."

Cindy looked at me, curled her lip. She told me she had eight horses of her own.

"*Eight?*" I said.

"I know horses," she said. "I know wild. Your horses are golf carts."

I protested. I tried to explain about Skippy. Cindy offered to come over one day and "freshen" our horses up. She made the point that our horses would probably prefer the riding life to the lazy days out there in the field with all the flies.

She showed up on a Thursday night with Bob and a bareback pad. She didn't believe in real saddles. Too much nonsense. She came from a cowgirl culture that said if you could ride bareback you could ride anything. She put a bridle on Blitz, threw the pad on his back, grabbed a hunk of mane, and hoisted herself up.

"Golf cart," Cindy said, steering him around. Yeah, well, I sort of knew Blitz was capable. She repeated the process with Maggie. "Golf cart," she said. "What is wrong with you people?"

"Mommy, I want to ride Maggie," Anna said.

"Can I wide Bitz?" Sasha said.

Soon enough we were all across the road, over at the round pen we hadn't even visited since those days when Alex broke his rib, and I was busily apologizing to Skippy for interrupting his days of grazing. Some of the boards had fallen loose but the basic structure was intact.

Anna had brought along a pad of paper and a marker, because this is what she does. When she is excited about something she has to either draw it or spell it. "How do we spell 'Maggie'?"

"Honey, you can ride her, but only if Cindy leads you around," I said.

"Oh, come on, Mom," Cindy said.

"She doesn't know how to ride bareback," I said.

Yes, apparently, she did. And so did Sasha. By the end of the evening, Cindy had both girls riding around our ring, nothing to it. Anna exuded the confidence of a queen, sitting straight and tall. Sasha approached Blitz much as she did swimming lessons. Just dive in there and go. Blitz is a fat pony, and Sasha is a short kid, the net result being she rode with her legs out as if doing a split. "Kick!" Cindy commanded. And Sasha's little ankles would barely pop up, but she'd manage to communicate her desire to go forward and Blitz would oblige. Soon Sasha was trotting around the pen to catch up with Anna, who was regally moving as if heading off to bestow gifts upon the king.

"I just can't believe this . . ." I said, repeatedly. My girls were *horse people*. And my horses were *people horses*. Here were all these pieces of the dream scattered about our big backyard, and here they were falling into a most glorious formation.

Skippy and I were standing together, watching Anna on Maggie and Sasha on Blitz, standing there together like two exlovers longing to dance. I was scratching his ear, which he loves.

"Aw, Skip," I said.

"Aw, sweetie," he said, but not in the way anyone else could hear.

Skippy has always had a thing for me, and I've always had a thing for him. Skippy is the mule version of my dog Betty, who is but the dog version of my first cat, Bob, and my second cat, Steve. All the pets I have bonded with, deeply and fully connected with, are the same beings, the same little souls. We are the type of friends who can pick up instantly with each other after years of separation.

Alex came up to the round pen, saw me and Skippy. "You two look good together," he said.

"Yeah, we do," I said.

It didn't take a lot more than that to convince me to climb on Skippy and see what would happen. I borrowed some of Sasha's courage and Anna's confidence. How strange to find this benefit of motherhood occurring so early. It was like having your kid turn into a lawyer or a doctor or a representative in pharmaceutical sales; you're the mom so you get free stuff.

"Okay, Skip," I said. "We're gonna do this. And this time no more Mrs. Nice Guy."

I climbed with some difficulty aboard. God, I'm old and creaky. God, my girls are young and supple. Skippy stood there, firm and solid, as I threw my leg over his back and then sat on him. Well, then. I had forgotten what his head looked like from this vantage point, his long ears like weeds in the breeze. "Good boy, Skip," I said, even though I was thinking, *Good job, Mom.* Then I squeezed my legs together and Skippy did it: he walked forward. I pulled back on the reins and Skippy stopped. Well, then!

"I swear he didn't do this six years ago when I tried!" I said to my little audience. "I *swear*! He's a changed mule!"

"Golf cart," Cindy said.

"Hey, girls!" I said. "Hey, look at me! How about me?" I thought Anna and Sasha would be thrilled to see their mom riding, but they were annoyingly more interested in their own achievements.

Alex was watching me. He was applauding, bless his heart. He knew how big a deal this was. And seeing Anna and Sasha going around with me. His whole family up there, having a happy horse life. I steered Skippy up to him, pulled back on the reins and stopped.

Alex stood there, all short and horseless. "You, my man," I said. "You need to get yourself a horse."

À Votre Santé, aka "Vortray": 2001 registered STB gelding, bay, 16.1+ hh (measured), sound for all professions, just didn't make a racehorse. Drives and rides. His sire is Jenna's Beach Boy and his dam is Christmas Wish. No allergies, no surgeries, fractures, injuries, or illnesses, no past lamenesses, nothing that would affect his ability to be ridden or driven. No behavioral quirks or vices, no feeding concerns or health problems, no areas where he is sensitive either physically or mentally, no traveling or conformational flaws. Current on all health care and shots. He is tattooed and branded. Pacing bred but prefers a trot, could go either way at this point, could do w/t/c or trained to be a gaited pleasure horse. We do have his registration papers and they will go with the adopter for showing purposes. Last driven on the track on 11/03, does everything that is asked of him (leads, loads, ties, cross-ties, bathes, clips), good in a diverse herd, great appetite, experienced shipper, has traveled from PA to

Florida and from Florida to Canada for training and yearling sales. Just a sponge waiting to be filled, ready for any job. Sweet boy that loves attention, very calm and loving horse for his age. Gets along well with everyone in our diverse group in turnout. Needs a family of his own. First couple of rides were a breeze. He'll be a beginner's horse in a month or two. We have Vortray's appraisal, he's been valued at $12,000. He has spent the last several months riding kids and beginners. Absolutely the best horse. Adoption fee is $3,000. There is a 20% discount if you can pay in full. I'm sure Vortray's owner had big hopes for him as a racehorse as he was bought as a yearling for a small fortune but not every horse has racing in their heart, he obviously had other plans. He's such a lover it's hard to imagine him having the competitive spirit but maybe racing just wasn't his thing.

Alex didn't want a racehorse, of course. No beginner wants to try to tackle a hot-blooded beast with an innate urge to run a million miles an hour around a track. But this was the horse we went to see after reading that online ad. And this is what we're towing home. À Votre Santé. "Vortray." Alex fell in love with him all on his own, really, with absolutely no help from me, but with the seal of approval from Cindy, who had agreed to come with us to look, and who had agreed to lend us her trailer, and who had said she herself wasn't going to get another horse, no way, there was no way in hell, she already had eight horses— eight horses!—and she didn't even have a house to live in yet, just a trailer, she really needed to go about building a house, and a life with Bob, and not spend her money or her energy or her commitment on another damn horse.

But the trailer she was lending us was a two-horse trailer. That was a fact.

Strong Fort, aka "Brego": 1994 TB gelding, 17.2 hands (measured), chestnut, imported from Ireland, former steeple-chaser, competed in Ireland and the U.S., sound but looking for a job on the flat or over fences or pleasure, preferably in a family situation with one rider, very sweet horse and easy to handle as long as you aren't feeding him a ton of sugar. Has some arthritis that shows up the first few steps out of the stall so we would like to have him not go into a heavy working or competition situation. Likes people, good manners, good with other animals, vet and farrier, loads and does everything asked of him on the ground. Outgoing and loves attention. Impressive good looks and amazing disposition! Adoption fee is $1,500. Absolutely a wonderful horse, a big dog type.

Brego was huge, a mass of muscle and kindness. Cindy was in love with him, tearing herself away. The barn we had traveled to was somewhere deep in godforsaken West Virginia, a mysterious place of fog and temptation.

There were dozens of horses in the barn for sale, all of them rescued animals, and the longer we stayed and shopped, the more the prices kept dropping. The barn was overcrowded and fall was coming; soon the owners would have trouble affording feed.

I watched Alex whisper what appeared to be sweet nothings into Vortray's ears. Tall and beefy and dopey, the horse wore a look that exactly said, "I *so* don't want to be a racehorse." Perhaps Alex was talking to him as he would his patients on the couch: *"There, there. It's okay. You shouldn't have to pretend to be someone you're not."*

Poor Vortray. According to his papers, his dad, Jenna's Beach Boy, had run the fastest one-mile trot of any horse, ever. And here he was the son, only four years old, and already a failure. A disgrace to the family line. Stuck in some godforsaken barn in godforsaken West Virginia, up for sale and the price dropping fast.

It was easy to romanticize the situation. Alex knew Vortray's story all too well: disgrace, failure, shame. Alex had disappointed his own dad, a mathematician famous in math circles. Alex was supposed to follow suit. Alex had little aptitude, even less interest in math. He chose to study religion, which his dad thought hogwash, and psychology, which his dad thought even worse. Alex came into adulthood knowing without a doubt that his dad thought him pathetic.

"I get you." That's what I imagined Alex saying to that big horse. *"I completely get you."* They looked good together. Vortray's nose was big and curved, like that of a Jewish man aging gracefully. Alex was a Jewish man aging gracefully. Vortray had big lumbering shoulders and soft eyes and the disposition of a man who didn't take himself too seriously. Alex was a man who didn't take himself too seriously.

When Alex finally climbed onto Vortray's back, and rode him calmly around the ring, I told him, I said, "You look good together."

"Go, Daddy!" Anna said.

"Dat!" Sasha screamed. "Can I try next?"

Cindy said we should take him. Cindy said let's get out of here. Cindy was tapping her foot.

Alex took out his checkbook. The owners had already offered to sell Vortray for nearly half of their asking price. Then they told Cindy they would throw in Brego for free.

"Free," Cindy said.

"He needs a good home and we think you're it," the woman said.

"Free," Cindy said. "You're offering to just *give* me this beautiful horse."

The woman shrugged.

"Bob," she said then. *"Bob!"*

"We can't do it," he said. "You know we can't."

She looked at Alex. Alex is a sucker for doe eyes. He had long since learned how to become blind to mine. But Cindy's, well, these were all new.

"We'll take Brego and keep him at our place," Alex said to me. "And Cindy can ride him when she comes over. What do you think?"

"Of course," I said. *Of course?* Two more horses—and gigantic ones, at that. *Of course?*

"Two horses!" Anna shouted. "I knew it! I knew we were going to get two horses!" She exploded into cartwheels. She needed a pen. And some paper. She needed to know how to spell "Vortray" and "Brego."

Now, I've heard about this horse phenomenon. I've heard it from Cindy and how she became a woman with eight horses and no house. Our farrier has fifteen horses and no time. Our vet has ten horses and no more room. Something happens to horse people. A gorging. An inability to say no. A welcoming spirit that has you imagining yourself throwing your arms around all the world's horses: *Come, my children, come.* I don't know exactly. But it was happening to us.

We walked Vortray and Brego to the trailer. My God, they were big. They were just . . . so damn big.

"You don't think they're too big?" I said to Alex.

"Well, they are . . . big," he said. We seemed to have trouble saying much else. We were in some sort of trance?

Poor Skippy, I thought. Oh, my poor little mule. Back home he was in charge of the herd, the master of all things, the one who decided who should have the most to eat (him) and the most to drink (him) and the coolest spot in the shade for snoozing (him). These two big galoots were sure to change the happy little society that was our farm.

" 'God is a comedian,' " Alex is saying, quoting Voltaire. " 'God is a comedian playing to an audience too afraid to laugh.' " The Voltaire kick is on account of the fact that he doesn't like the name Vortray, so maybe he should rename his horse Voltaire. He has decided that this is too pretentious, but he has not stopped quoting Voltaire.

We are sick of Voltaire. We are sick of each other. I can't move. It has taken us four hours to get here, to the intersection of Wilson Road and our driveway. The horses have grown. In my mind they turned first into giraffes and then elephants and soon enough into woolly mammoths.

I can't believe we're doing this. I can't believe no one is saying, "I can't believe we're doing this."

I can't move. Anna is snoring. Sasha's head is so hot. My left leg is numb from some pinched nerve and this entire extended cab smells like salami due to the fact that Sasha did not, apparently, eat her sandwich but rather rolled it up and stuffed it in the cup holder just out of my reach.

"Well, we made it," Alex says as we pull into the driveway, inch down the hill. He's all cheerful. He's all high on horse acquisition. He's wondering what the heck is going on as the truck sputters, chugs, sputters, stops dead. Right in the middle of the driveway. We are about one hundred yards from the house, and we are out of gas.

God is a comedian.

"This, I cannot deal with," Alex says, throwing the door open. "I'm leaving the truck here until morning."

"Please, let us out," Cindy says.

Alex and Cindy and Bob hop out and leave me trapped back here with the snoozing lumps. I hear the clunking and "hep! hepping!" of horses being unloaded from the trailer and the horses finally emerge, remarkably calm, both of them seeming to have survived this trip better than any of us. *Big. Oh, my God. Big horses.* Will they even fit? Will they trample the trees and will their feet put giant cracks in the earth causing mass flooding?

Cindy and Alex and Bob usher the horses into the back field. Within seconds those monsters charge, disappearing up the hill and into the fog that promises to lift, a curtain to some kind of strange tomorrow.

nothing surprises
me anymore

NAIROBI, Kenya (AP)—A NURSING DOG FORAGING FOR
FOOD RETRIEVED AN ABANDONED BABY GIRL IN A FOREST
IN KENYA AND CARRIED THE INFANT TO ITS LITTER OF
PUPPIES, WITNESSES SAID MONDAY.

May 9, 2005

The stray dog carried the infant across a busy road and a barbed wire fence in a poor neighborhood near the Ngong Forests in the capital, Nairobi, Stephen Thoya told the independent Daily Nation *newspaper.*

The dog apparently found the baby Friday in the plastic bag in which the infant had been abandoned, said Aggrey Mwalimu, owner of the compound where the animal is now living. It was unclear how the baby survived in the bag without suffocating.

Doctors said the baby had been abandoned about two days before the dog discovered her. Medical workers later found maggots in the infant's umbilical cord, a product of days of neglect, Hannah Gakuo, the spokeswoman of the Kenyatta National Hospital, where the girl was taken for treatment, said Monday. No one has yet claimed the baby, she said.

But the 3.3 kilogram (7.28 pounds) infant "is doing well, responding to treatment, she is stable . . . she is on antibiotics," Gakuo told the Associated Press. Workers at the hospital are calling the child Angel, she said.

I keep rereading this article, thinking I should be more impressed. Who doesn't love a story like this? Young man raised by wolves returns to civilization and becomes U.S. senator, or some such.

Nothing surprises me anymore, at least when it comes to birth, death, and so much of the action in between. Who gave birth to whom, which is raising what. I've got a sheep raised by goats, who just had twins and rejected one, which now my daughters are raising, bottle-feeding little Emily four times a day. I've got a pregnant donkey that should have delivered three months ago, so now we think she isn't pregnant, but everyone, including the vet, says, "Just give it a few more weeks." I've got twenty-five baby chicks due to arrive in the mail this Thursday, an overreaction on my part to waking up one morning and finding that we had forgotten to shut the door of the chicken coop one night, so a raccoon came and gobbled up Penelope and Magenta, our two favorite hens.

I'm jaded. Who gave birth to whom, which is raising what,

who killed what and how. I'm glad the dog in Nairobi found that baby. Sure, I am. And I think it's great she was evolved enough to know to do the right thing. For her sake I do sort of wish she had been allowed a little more time with the infant, that she got more of a chance to wow us with her intraspecies mothering skills. But, hey, happily-ever-after is happily-ever-after, so of course I'm glad Angel got the antibiotics.

I'm jaded. And I'm upset about the chickens. That was so depressing. All that was left of Penelope were a few buff-colored feathers, and all that was left of Magenta was a leg. The raccoon was still up in the maple tree. Apparently, Marley had been let out before daybreak and heard the raccoon before it had a chance to return to the woods, and he chased it up the tree. John, the guy who sometimes comes to cut our grass, and his nephew, Mike, who was repairing our roof, said we had to shoot the raccoon.

"We?" I said.

And soon enough John went home to get the rifles and then he and Mike stood under the tree and aimed up while I covered my ears.

Death, birth, joy, abandonment, adoption, rescue, hunt, blood, guts, corpse, chicken leg on the patio. Nothing surprises me anymore. All of this stuff is pretty normal. Back where I grew up, in the suburbs, it wasn't normal. At the Babies "R" Us baby store, and Pottery Barn Kids, it still isn't normal. In the typical modern mind, babies are born and mothers are happy and girlfriends bring presents and everyone sits around marveling at adorable tiny outfits until they get on to the business of building toy wagons and, later, bikes. Parenting is a wonderful thing and a surprisingly difficult thing but it is always more or less, in our minds, linear.

The farm has taught me differently. It has taught my daughters differently. It is, at least, one explanation as to why my girls seem so thoroughly uninterested in their own adoption stories. Who gave birth to whom, which is raising what. They're jaded. I read all the time of adoptive moms having all sorts of elaborate and philosophical discussions with their kids about the adoption experience. These conversations are said to begin as early as age three. I am wide open to these discussions. I have rehearsed them in my mind countless times. When the time is right I will plunge right in. I keep thinking there will be a question, some curiosity, some . . . anxiety or some need to know something. Since the beginning we've talked about them being born in China, then adopted by us. The bare bones story is part of their basic memory. Over time I've cleared up the misconception that China is, simply, where babies come from. No, I tell them, babies come from women's bellies. And the women with the bellies live all over the world. *Big?* Yes, honey, the bellies are big. *Big like the belly on the sheep with the crooked neck?* Yes, honey, as big as that and sometimes even bigger.

We watched the sheep with the crooked neck give birth on Mother's Day, of all days. That was a gift. Or, it started out as one. She was our last sheep to deliver, having gone into labor, finally, and several weeks after the others, most probably late because of all she had been through. On a brutally cold February night, that poor girl had found herself in the teeth of coyotes. She nearly died, and would have if Luna, our livestock guardian dog, hadn't done what her breed had been bred for thousands of years to do: save its charges from the jaws of predators. Luna had been out there barking since dawn. From the window we could see the sheep, and so we counted, as we usually do. There were six instead of seven. Alex climbed onto his ATV and went charging. He found that ewe there, a bloody lump, still breathing. Without intervention, a coyote would have finished the job. A coyote would have dragged her kill back to the pack and the feast would have happened and then they all would have slept peacefully with their satisfied stomachs.

Even George had to admit it, when Alex called him and he came over to help get the sheep down off the hill and into a pen in the barn. George didn't believe in livestock guardian dogs but now he believed in Luna. She had scared the coyote off; it had to have happened that way. There would have been no other reason for the coyote to leave.

For days the sheep lay in the pen, motionless but still breathing. We shot her up with antibiotics. The wounds were all around her neck, deep in the muscles. She never acquired an infection. In a few weeks she stood. We were all there when she took her first bite of grain, and we clapped and sang songs. We kept her in the pen all winter. In the spring she got her own private outdoor pen. We kept watch over her. Amazingly, she seemed to have kept the baby growing inside her; all signs showed that she was just as pregnant as the other ewes. The wounds around her neck healed, but the neck itself wasn't quite right. She held her head low and crooked, as if the ligaments were too short on one side, or as if she didn't quite know what to make of life, having suffered her near-death experience.

She became "the sheep with the crooked neck."

So, finally, on Mother's Day she was out in the pen, pacing, pawing at the ground, and soon enough we saw a little lamb hoof sticking out. We pulled up some bricks, all four of us, each with our own little brick to sit on, and watched. "What a thrill!" I said to the girls. I told them it was my first time ever seeing anything being born and this was a special day indeed. We sat there waiting. And waiting. Skippy came over and stood with us. And then an hour went by and still there was just the foot and so the girls got bored so they fed Skippy some apple treats. Another hour went by and even Skippy got bored. Sasha went and got her new pink beach ball and we started kicking and soon enough I was teaching the girls everything I knew about soccer, which wasn't much. We kicked and kicked and the sun was going down and Alex never left the sheep.

It was after eight and getting dark and all that was sticking out was a leg, so I took the girls in for dinner. Alex came in about a half hour later and said the lamb was born, that all at once it was born, a perfect little lamb, fully formed and adorable as any baby animal God ever invented, except it was dead.

There it was. Expectation, birth, death. All in one tidy little package with a game of soccer thrown in, not to mention a coyote attack and a heroic dog rescue.

The girls were more confused than upset. Why was the lamb dead? What would we do with it? Would it go to heaven and join all of our other dead animals, and how would it get there?

I was glad they were asking. I don't know if my answers were any good, but the fact that they were asking gave me hope. I want to be one of those mothers who have "good communication" with her daughters. I want them to be able to ask me any-thing, to share fear and doubt and anger and joy. The fact that they never ask about their own adoption stories has me concerned on this front.

On the night of the stillborn lamb, there was disappointment, the emptiness of failure, but no tears were shed for the lamb that never got a chance at life. It was, simply, the cycle of life, and this one never quite got spinning. My girls were fine with that. They had seen enough of death and life to be fine with that. All babies come out of women's bellies. Some of them make it out alive and some of them don't and some of them stay from day one with the one who gave birth to them, and some go on to be raised by other moms, goats and sister ducks and dogs. My girls know this as well as they know that chickens lay eggs and sometimes we eat the eggs and sometimes the hens sit on the eggs until they hatch into chicks.

Sometimes, when I'm driving, I hear them in the back discussing the subject.

"Ladies have babies in she bellies," Sasha said one day, in her Sasha-speak.

"*Their* bellics," Anna said, "and it's not all ladies. Some do, and some don't."

"They come out the poop," Sasha said.

"That's disgusting. It's not in the poop, Sasha."

"They come out she bummy," Sasha said.

"*Her* bummy," Anna said. "And not all ladies have babies in them anyway."

"That's true," I said, chiming in. "I never had a baby in my belly."

"You never had one?" Anna said.

"Nope."

Now we were getting somewhere. I felt the tiniest twinge of excitement. Maybe we were going to do the full adoption talk now. Maybe they were ready with their questions.

"We came from China," Sasha said.

"That's right," I said. "And not out of my belly."

"That's right," Sasha said.

And why weren't they asking who, exactly, gave birth to them? Why had this question not yet occurred to them? It's the question adoptive parents like me figure will be the central issue of our kids' lives. It's the question our kids will spend their lives wondering about. Isn't it? And it's my duty to prepare them. Isn't it? I'm supposed to feed them all the information I have now, early on, so when the questions really start firing, the doubt and the fear, they'll have a good leg up on making sense of the trauma. Aren't I? This is how the moms in my adoption magazines seem to have it worked out. Only, they seem to have kids who ask, who are curious, who have by age three already mastered the word "birth-mother" and the concept of a mother who came before.

What was wrong with my kids? Why weren't they asking the question?

"Girls, you both came out of bellies," I said, as if to gently fuel the fire. "Just not out of mine."

"Well, who did you come out of?" Anna asked.

Who did I come out of? Oh, for heaven's sakes. That wasn't the way this was supposed to go. I wanted to talk about their "birth-mothers." It's not a term I would choose, but I know it will be one they'll hear in school, so they might as well have it as part of their vocabulary.

"Honey, you know Grandmom was my birth-mother," I said. "And she raised me. But not all birth-mothers raise their kids. Sometimes babies are adopted, like you girls were."

"Was Grandmom really fat?" Anna asked.

"Huh?"

"When you were in her belly."

"Sure, sweetie. I mean, I don't remember, but I think so."

Then finally I just forced the issue. "I don't know the ladies who gave birth to you girls," I said. "Do you understand that? I never met either of your birth-mothers and I don't think we ever will."

"Well, do you know if mine was fat?" Anna said.

I was getting a headache. I actually had to take my finger and push that spot on my right temple that I could feel throbbing, diffusing the pain through my hand and down my arm where it eventually got absorbed. I was not one of those mothers who had "good communication" with her daughters. I just wasn't, although it wasn't for lack of trying.

"She was probably fat," I said. "At least right before she had you. Most ladies with babies in them are."

"My lady was fat, too?" Sasha said.

"Probably."

That was it. The conversation drifted almost immediately over to a discussion of where, exactly, Care Bears come from. I didn't know the answer. "The sky, Mommy," Anna said. Duh. "That's why they have the rainbow sliding board?"

Duh.

I drove around thinking how complicated stories of birth can be. Who gave birth to whom, which is raising what. This is what my girls are used to. This is where they start. To make their own stories stand out would be to deny a complexity they have come to depend on.

As for the sheep with the crooked neck, she survived her tragedy, more or less. On the night she gave birth to her failed promise, I went out to visit her before I went to bed. Alex had already taken the stillborn lamb away. The mom was standing in the pen, her head to one side, and she was hollering for her lamb; instinct tells her to holler "Meeeh!" until the baby answers.

"I'm sorry, girl," I said. "I'm so sorry." Not a personal sorry but certainly a compassionate one. "You did a good job," I assured her. "You did all you could do."

"Meeeh!"

I had no idea how to console a sheep, with or without a crooked neck, and I stood there under the moonlight thinking, stupidly, that I probably shouldn't say anything to her at all about it being Mother's Day.

Now, dogs, as anyone knows, are about a million times more evolved than sheep. I keep thinking about that dog in Nairobi. I keep insisting that I'm not impressed by the rescue, and yet I can't stop thinking about that dog.

Now, dogs, if they are so highly evolved, should be able to talk. I've held this belief for a long time, especially in regard to Betty, my twelve-year-old mutt. Whole days go by with her at my feet, underneath my desk, or beside me snoring, and we have long conversations with one another until I realize, wait a second, she isn't actually talking, is she? No, she is not. Although of course she is speaking. I mean, I can hear her. The speaking is through her eyes and her expressions and the tilting of her chin and the sigh she has always been famous for. Or, before a storm, long before I can hear the thunder, the jiggle of her nervous little body, aquiver with fear over the arrival of some monster she can't otherwise articulate.

"It's okay, girly," I'll say.

Sometimes, of course, no storm comes and Betty continues her quivering and I'll have no idea what the problem is.

"What? *What?*"

But she responds with just more of the same, a lot of jiggling and words I can only imagine. I don't think it's fair. Dogs have so much going for them, they should have words. If they had words they could tell stories. They could sing. They could paint pictures and have art shows. Wouldn't it be wonderful if just one other species besides us had the gift of self-expression?

There are those who think animals do, or imagine they do, or hope. You read all the time of people holding out for the real story of all that dolphin chatter. That's not what I'm talking about. I'm talking jokes. I'm talking Broadway shows written by and starring dogs. I'm talking art shows with dog art critics who aren't super dogs, just regular dogs. Homeless dogs at the pound and Park Avenue poodles who go about their days chowing down on Alpo in their stainless steel bowls, but they also use the phone and call their friends and schedule outings.

But maybe I'm just elevating the spoken word to a status it

doesn't deserve. Millions of species have probably a million ways of communicating that we'll never understand.

I knew two old lady identical twins who lived together and one did the shopping and if the other needed chicken soup while the sister was already at the store, all she would have to do was think *chicken soup, chicken soup* and sure enough the sister would throw a few cans in the cart.

Skeptics doubt me when I tell them about those twins, but it's usually an easier sell than explaining the communication I have with my dog. One night, seemingly out of nowhere, I got the sense that something was wrong with Betty. I was just sitting there watching *Jeopardy!* and I thought, *Where's Betty?* I stood out on the porch and called her. Usually one "Betty!" followed by a high-pitched "Weee-oooo!" will yield the sound of her dog tag clanking and soon enough I'll see her little blonde self come prancing up the path.

But not this time. Maybe she was just busy sniffing in the woods or wasn't quite finished chewing a stick—these things happened. But I couldn't let go of the sense that something was wrong with her.

"Betty!" I yelled. I could see all the way down to the barn. The moon was out by then, bright as a spotlight. This was one of those amazing facts of country life: You could do needle-point under a moon like that.

"Betty!" I walked up our road, then down the path to the small pond in our back field.

"Betty!"

This was crazy. Why wasn't she answering? This was not like

her. I continued walking and then, in the stillness, I heard something. A kind of chirp.

"Betty?"

"Eeet!"

I walked in the direction of the chirp. It was in the woods? Or back up on the road? On such a still night, echoes play tricks. "Beeetty!"

"Eeet!"

She was calling me. Why was it such a pathetically weak call?

"Beeeettty!"

"Eeet!"

The sound was coming from the top of our steep hill. Walking up that hill, you usually have to take breaks to catch your breath. But this time I ran straight up, like a lady lifting a car off her kid. "I'm coming, girly! I'm coming!"

I found her under a naked maple tree, her little body vibrating crazily. "What? *What?*" I ran to her and threw my arms around her and saw that her leg was caught in the jaws of a coyote trap that some idiot had taken the liberty of setting on our property.

"Oh, girly!" I had no idea how to release a coyote trap. I used my fingernails to try and dig its anchor out of the ground, and then I got a stick. "How long have you been up here? How did this happen? Oh, sweetie."

Of course, I got her out. I hugged her and carried her down the hill. Her leg was bruised and cut, but it would heal just fine. Had I not found her and freed her, I don't know what would have happened. Would she have been easy bait for a pack of coyotes? Would she have chewed her own leg off to get free? You hear about that sort of thing. You hear about men trapped under fallen trees and cutting off their own feet. "Oh, girly." All night long and forever after that I wondered how Betty was able to get my attention, get me outside there looking for her. How? How in the name of Alex Trebek did she let me know? It was a feeling in my skin, a smell, or maybe something in the wind. The only thing I'm sure it wasn't was the spoken word.

Fortunately, that was the last in a long line of mishaps for Betty. The bee stings that nearly killed her, the time she cut her paw on a chunk of glass and nearly bled to death in the creek. On average, Betty has suffered through two traumatic events per year for most of her life. The coyote trap might have been her swan song. After that she stuck closer to home, most days under my desk, where we have our conversations, discuss current events, and sometimes get into debates. But usually we agree. Really, we see the world remarkably similarly.

I was just talking to her about that dog in Nairobi who found the baby.

"You keep saying you're not impressed, and yet you keep talking about it," she said.

"That's exactly my point," I said.

She was lying on her back with her feet sticking straight up in the air, a posture of approval. Then she said: "Well, did they give that dog the chance to say goodbye to the kid?"

"I don't know, girly," I said. "I do not know."

"Well," she wisely observed, "I'm sure it was an emotional time for everybody."

Betty is already older than me. In dog years she's about the age of my mom. She listens better than my mom, and certainly better than my kids. It takes years of togetherness to get like this.

Now they're saying Sasha doesn't have apraxia. They're saying that, anyway, the original diagnosis was "mild" apraxia, and now that they see how quickly Sasha is acquiring speech, they don't believe the apraxia diagnosis was accurate.

"Quickly?" I said.

She was still largely unintelligible to anyone but those of us who spent our days with her and knew how to translate Sasha-speak.

They said in her recent tests she could, at age four, form all the sounds of a profoundly delayed three-year-old, which was certainly not good, but wasn't consistent with apraxia.

"So what do you think it is?" I said to Miss Joy, the speech therapist Sasha had been seeing three times a week for the previous nine months.

She shrugged. "There's so much we don't know." I wasn't sure if she was referring to the speech therapy industry or perhaps to Sasha's earliest months in the orphanage where who-knows-what happened that might have so severely interrupted her ability to acquire language.

It didn't matter. The therapists simply didn't know what was wrong, but the good news was Sasha now spoke the garbled language of hope. "With my young apraxic kids," Miss Joy said, "I can't get any of the sounds out of them that Sasha is now able to produce." She was recommending we stop therapy for about six months, see what she was able to do on her own, and then retest her. Her guess was that Sasha had been through the worst of it, that her little brain had finally begun to figure this language thing out, and that we would now see tremendous progress.

"We see this sometimes," she said. "All of a sudden something clicks, like an engine that finally turned over, and pretty soon everything is running fine."

"So it's just like . . . an ignition problem? Like she just needed a new starter?"

"Sort of."

She gave us some exercises to do, most of them involving sentence structure since, inexplicably, Sasha couldn't seem to master certain sequences. "The boy is running" came out "The boy running" or "The boy is run." Ask her to do the verb with the "ing" and she got completely flummoxed.

So we were supposed to do drills. We were supposed to work on pronouns. We were supposed to pretend not to understand her when she jumbled syllables, flipped words haphazardly this way and that inside a sentence.

"You have to insist that she speak *our* language, not hers," Miss Joy told us.

"You don't think I'll be stifling her creativity?" I said.

"Uh, no," Miss Joy said. "No."

Right, then. Of course. Stupid question. Where did that

come from? Whew. Parents go either one way or the other on this one, I think. There are those who regard their children as lanky, crazy vines that need to be tacked onto trellises, pruned, trained to grow straight and tall and to bloom their maximum blooms seasonally, and on command.

And then there are those of us who stand in awe, so amazed by what we see growing in so many ways we could have never imagined, that we are humbled and afraid to inflict our own idiotic ideas upon the process. I'd been having a lot of awe attacks with regard to Sasha.

We shared cookies and juice with Miss Joy, a little goodbye party, and then Sasha gave Miss Joy a potted geranium. "Woo yike it?" she said to Miss Joy, who nodded enthusiastically and hugged her. "I love it," she said. "And I love you, too, sweetie."

"I wuff woo," Sasha said, throwing her arms around her and planting a kiss on her left eye.

"Awwww," said the gathered crowd of therapists. "Awwww, she is so sweet!"

Sweet. This is Sasha's gift. It isn't really about being sweet. It's about winning. This is her game. She came up with this one all on her own—and maybe her lack of language had something to do with it. I don't know. But Sasha can make anyone feel like a million bucks. She knows exactly how to do it and she has made of it something of a fine art.

Her usual targets are women, although she can easily enough work the magic on men. It happens at parties, or the playground, or whenever she is in a safe place with a cast of at least vaguely familiar characters. She'll pick one. She'll hold her arms up. "Up! Up!" she'll say, her posture pleading and pathetic and convincing. The person will say, "Me?" The person will say, "Aw." The person will look at me to see if it's okay if they pick her up and I'll nod. Soon she will be in the person's arms. She will look that person in the eye, and sometimes will place one hand on each cheek, grabbing full attention.

"Woo," she will say. "I yike woo."

Anybody can translate that. Anybody. And each of the anybodies are transformed into *somebodies*, right then and there, thanks to Sasha. They glow. They have been *chosen*. They hug her. "Aww." They tell her how sweet she is. They go about their days feeling special. (And she just got a ride from here to there, on somebody's hip.)

Sasha has thus charmed preschool teachers and swimming instructors and dry cleaner clerks and even, for my sake, a judge at traffic court who let me off with a smile. She is my secret weapon and she knows it and so I have to be careful. She and I, we could be criminals together, like in *Paper Moon*. We could sell Bibles to Sunday School teachers and simultaneously clean out the church coffers. She could dance a jig for the pharmacist while I slip in the back and steal the drugs. It's not good to imagine entering a life of crime with your kid, no, there is nothing good you can say about it. But when you have a kid who knows how to turn on the charm this well, your dreams go into overdrive.

She is the only reason the principal at school is nice to me, if you can call making eye contact nice. It's a big step for Miss Martha, an ex-nun with a military haircut who might have had a very promising career in the marines, or else in the air force piloting fast planes with explosives. She is a serious woman dedicated to order, one of those people who can make you feel like a slob on impact. Sasha knows how to get through. Sasha will hold her skinny little arms up, pathetically. "Up! Up!" It's all so urgent and pitiful even Miss Martha can't resist, so she will pick Sasha up. And so Sasha will go at her with her cheek, and an embrace, until she has that cheek locked right there on Miss Martha's jaw. The lady can't help but melt. "Aw," Miss Martha will say, awkwardly. "Aw."

"Woo nice yay-yay," Sasha will say, which in Sasha-speak translates to "You're a nice lady." She says this in such a way as to suggest that she does not say it to virtually every person who answers her pathetic plea to carry her, which she does.

"Well, thank you," Miss Martha will reply. You can tell the inner nice lady dying to get out has just been activated. She'll smile broadly in a way that makes her face look grotesque, so unused to the position is that face.

Sasha will simply rest her head on Miss Martha's shoulder, and sometimes she'll give her a little pat on the back. Onlookers will actually gasp at the transformation, and I'll stand there watching, feeling not exactly proud, but certainly inspired. *God, Sasha's got that lady so transfixed I could probably go into her office and root through her files . . .* I'll find myself thinking, shifting into opportunist mode, a clever fox, and then I'll snap out of it. *Sasha, what are you doing to me? What do you do to people? You can hardly even talk and yet you have the power to convert.*

Sasha has, I know, a very promising political career, and I am doing everything I can to stay on her good side.

A few days ago, my mother sent me an e-mail:

```
guess what  for the first time in years i
did a little pastel of sasha @ her lamb not
great but not bad considering the
difficulties i had finding my pastels and
making do  ,hard to see the details  i will
try again  how about me_
```

This came through in 18-point type, her default setting because she has so much trouble with her eyes. My mother isn't much of a typist. She is eighty-two. She might be eighty-three. She can't remember. She'd have to ask my father if you really wanted to know. Details have never been her thing.

A whole new relationship has emerged between my mom and me ever since she got the computer, her first. She is now Mrs. E-mail. Her favorite thing to do is to send animated greeting cards. If she sees a good one that happens to be, say, a Father's Day card, she'll e-mail it to me anyway and tell me to just go on and ignore the greeting and watch the dancing duck.

"Cool!" I'll write to her. "Thanks!"

Then she'll call me and we'll discuss the transaction. How cute the duck is. How amazing it is that she knew how to send an e-card. The minor technical difficulties conquered. I'll tell her how great she is. How proud I am of her. We'll hang up and an hour later I'll get another.

"Did you get that one?" she'll say, calling to verify. "Did you get it?"

"Mom, you don't have to call," I'll say, trying to explain. "It kind of defeats the purpose."

"But I'm excited!" she'll say. "Isn't this amazing? Can you believe how good I am at this crazy computer?"

I'll tell her how great she is. How proud I am of her. This has been the classic mother/daughter role reversal. Nothing I ever accomplished was complete without my mom's approval. I suppose it's still this way, but now she needs me, too.

One morning she called to discuss her success at downloading a batch of photos I sent of the girls. She loved the one of Sasha feeding Emily. She spoke of printing it, even forwarding it. Another challenge! She said the thing about the computer was it got her living again. "I'm alive when I'm learning," she said. "And there's so much to learn about this dumb thing."

Summers when I was home from grad school we would talk like this, about living to learn. We were so busy. She was studying painting at a fancy fine-arts college, and I was trying to write stories. I worked upstairs in the little yellow bedroom and she painted down in her studio. We would meet at lunchtime for tuna and iced tea and we would marvel at the similarities between a blank page and a blank canvas. When it came to the creative process, fear was fear, no matter what the medium. We would suffer this fact together, cheer each other on. "Just go make a mess," one of us would say, before heading back to our separate rooms. Scribble anything. That was the way in.

That was a million years ago. My mom stopped painting when her legs and hips gave out on her, then her eyes. My sisters and brother and I nagged for years, and she made a few efforts. She'd painted portraits of all her grandchildren, and when Anna came along she made sure to do a little picture, if only for the sake of tradition. But by the time Sasha came, well, that was after the disease that temporarily paralyzed my mom, and after the breast cancer, and after the hip surgery, after her eyes went. My mom's health was way too far gone to paint.

"This photo makes me want to paint," she said to me a few days ago when I sent the photo of Sasha and the lamb.

"So go paint," I said. She made her excuses. I told her I was going up to my office to crank out one thousand words and if I could do it, she could, too. "Go make a mess," I said.

This kind of talking is the best communication my mom and I have ever mastered. It's the most genuine and the most productive. It's two people fundamentally understanding one another, and fundamentally wanting to help. Maybe this is as good as it gets between a mom and a daughter. You have one subject you really excel at, can communicate about with a wink and a nod and little more than a buzz phrase, and then the rest of your talking is a lot of noise back and forth, a content-free ritual keeping you connected.

Shortly after I told my mother to "go paint," I got the e-mail announcing that she had. It came through at about five in the afternoon. I wrote back with a lot of exclamation points, telling her to scan the painting and send it to me. She called immediately. She said she didn't know how to scan a picture. I gave her a few tips.

So then I got a new e-mail, with an attachment. I clicked and saw Sasha, through my mother's eyes. She was set against a field of green, and her head was leaning in toward the lamb, a tilt that was utterly Sasha. I felt like dancing.

My mom called me right away. "Did you get it? Did you get it?" she said.

"I got it!"

"So how about me!" she said. "I can scan a picture!" She went on about the difference between a JPEG and a TIFF format and how she chose.

"Mom," I said. "The *painting*. You painted a picture. Hello?"

"Oh," she said. "It's not up to my standards. But I knew you'd like it."

I told her I loved it. I told her how proud I was of her. I went on and on trying to convince her to frame the picture, to take it around to show her friends at the retirement village.

"We'll see," she said. "I'll look at it in the morning with a fresh eye. Maybe throw some darks in."

"Well, I think you should congratulate yourself," I said. "This is really an accomplishment."

"Right."

She was remarkably unimpressed with herself, or maybe I was hyping the whole deal too much, embarrassing her.

"Thank you, Mom," I said. "It really means a lot to me that you painted a picture of Sasha."

"You're welcome, dear. Now leave me alone."

"All right."

"Everything else okay?" she said. "The girls are okay? Alex?"

"Everyone's good. Hey, did you get my e-mail?"

"I couldn't open it," she said. "It was something about a dog?"

"Yeah, it was an article about a dog in Nairobi," I said. "You didn't read it?"

"I clicked but I couldn't get anything to happen," she said.

"Well, there was a stray dog in Nairobi and she found an infant in a garbage bag and dragged it back to her litter and took care of it."

"The baby is alive?"

"Yeah, they named her Angel."

"God must have plans for her. God was looking out for her."

"Yeah, but what about the dog, Mom? The *dog*."

"You have always been an animal person," she said.

"Oh, God."

"Sweetie, don't take the Lord's name in vain."

"The dog! How about that dog!"

"How do they know the dog really did it? Someone stood around and watched? That's odd . . ."

"You have always been a cynic."

"*Skeptic.*"

"Well, I don't know how they know it happened," I said. "But it happened. And I can't stop thinking about the dog. It's like a song playing over and over again in my head."

"You have always been an animal person."

"It's more complicated than that . . ."

"I'm tired, sweetie. I'm glad about the Nigerian baby, really I am."

"Nairobi," I said. "And I was more thinking about the dog."

"Well, it's nice to hear some good news once in a while. Your father and I are so sick of all the bad news on TV."

Right. Whatever. Some daughters are good at being heard, whereas others should have just stopped back at "Waaah!"

It's okay. This is all okay and par for the course and everything that I'm used to. I learned long ago that my mother would never really understand me. I learned not to go to her with problems, or doubt, because she can't sit in problems, or doubt. She has to fix things. This is probably true for most good moms. It goes back to Band-Aids. The kid is crying, you have to pick her up and make her feel better. But sometimes a kid really does need to just sit in doubt, to wonder, and sob. This wasn't exactly what I was feeling about the dog in Nairobi. I just wanted, I don't know, to talk.

"Hey, what about your birthday?" my mother said. "Anything special I can get you?"

Oh, jeez. My birthday was only a week away and I really hadn't had time to think about it.

"Anything you want?" she said.

Well, I had no idea. It seemed a strangely monumental question. I'd been so busy. My life was feeling like a Venn diagram of intersecting tasks. One big mess of responsibilities. "You know what," I said finally, "I just don't have time to want anything."

"Oh," she said. "Well, that's wonderful!"

Wonderful? To be too busy to know what the heck you'd like for your own birthday? "I'm not sure it's wonderful," I said. "What do you mean, wonderful?"

"If you're too busy to think about wanting, it means you're leading a full life," she said, throwing out one of her maxims.

"If you're too busy to think about wanting," I corrected her, "it means . . . you're *too busy*. It's not good to be too busy. People need downtime. People need to remember to *play*, smell the roses and all like that."

"A lot of people are very busy wanting," she said.

Maybe. I wondered why she was hammering the point. Was this some sneaky way of getting out of buying me a stinkin' birthday present? No. My mother doesn't sneak. And she loves to buy presents.

"People spend all their time wanting more and more," she said, "thinking that's the answer to happiness. But *you* know that the wanting train goes nowhere. That's why I'm proud of you."

Oh, brother. She had me way elevated beyond my original point. This virtuous me she was conjuring was not, well, me.

"Mom, I don't have the *energy* to get on the wanting train," I said. "Do you understand what I'm saying?"

"I do!" she said.

"I'm saying that in order to open the ol' boxcar of personal desire," I said, choosing my words very carefully so as not to be misunderstood, "I'd have to find a way to *stop* this barreling locomotive I seem to have gotten myself on."

"You have always been so good with metaphors!"

Oh, my God! Were we even having the same conversation?

"I never got you very many Christmas presents," she said,

ridiculously veering off, as a mother does, to mother-guilt. "I'm sorry. I just didn't want you kids to grow up thinking that material goods were the answer."

"I always wanted more Christmas presents," I told her. "I always wanted more."

"But look at you now!"

"*Oh, my God!*"

"Why do you have to take the Lord's name in vain?"

"I'm sorry."

I gave up. Because there's no sense arguing with your own mother over the point that you are not quite as swell as she has you made out to be. It would be like your dog trying to convince you that it's not the most adorable little pooch to walk the face of this earth—a waste of that dog's slobber.

This, I think, might be the main communication breakdown between mothers and daughters. The mother is programmed to see the kid as wonderful. She cannot hear the other stuff. It's not her fault. You, as kid, are her accomplishment. You are the product of all those years and years of her hard labor. You are her best work of art.

And if you love her, really love her, you'll give her this. You may not see the beauty. You may feel like hell. But if you love her, really love her, you'll give her this. "Yay, me." You'll keep your problems to yourself. You won't show doubt or fear or, Lord knows, any of the anger you feel for not finding your voice with her, for not being known.

And now here I sit. Here I sit wanting to be one of those mothers who have "good communication" with their daughters. I want my girls to be able to ask me anything, to wonder aloud with me about their own adoption stories, to ask me to simply sit with them while they howl in pain. And where in the world do I suppose I'll find the strength to become one of those mothers? *Where in the world?*

"Well, you sure did a good job raising me," I said to my mom that day, hoping to wrap this one up.

"I could have gotten you more Christmas presents," she said. "Really, what would have been the harm?"

"Oh my God, Mom, let it go! You did a great job."

"Thank you. But you really shouldn't take the Lord's name in vain, sweetie."

Offers to Adopt Baby Rescued by Stray Dog

HOSPITAL OFFICIALS SAY PEOPLE EAGER TO HELP ABANDONED NEWBORN

The Associated Press
Updated: 3:21 p.m. ET, May 10, 2005

NAIROBI, Kenya—*Offers to adopt a newborn girl found among a litter of puppies after being abandoned are pouring in to the Kenyan hospital where she is being treated, and the stray dog credited with her rescue has a home and a name—"Mkombozi" or "Savior."*

As police searched for the infant's mother, a government spokesman expressed some skepticism Tuesday about the story of the dog's role in saving the child, dubbed "Angel" by hospital workers, and said authorities were investigating.

"I saw a dog carrying a baby wrapped in a black dirty cloth as it crossed the road," witness Stephen Thoya was quoted by the

independent Daily Nation *newspaper as saying. "I was shocked at first, and when I tried to get a closer look, the dog ran through the fence and disappeared along a dirt road."*

The infant was discovered after two children alerted adults that they heard the sound of a baby crying near their wooden and corrugated-iron shack. Residents found the baby lying next to the dog and her own pup.

"One of those amazing things"

Government spokesman Alfred Mutua said authorities were investigating the rescue story.

"This is a very interesting development and the government is looking into it because if it happened the way it has been relayed, it is one of those amazing things that happens in life that defies human explanation," he said. "It indicates that there is somebody out there watching over us."

Well-wishers from Kenya and as far as the United States have sent e-mails to the Associated Press and called the country's main hospital to inquire about adopting the child.

Dog gets a new home

The stray dog that saved the child also was being cared for Tuesday, a day after its last surviving puppy died for unknown reasons, said Jean Gilchrist of the Kenya Society for the Protection and Care of Animals.

"She looks a bit depressed so we'd like to examine her to see if she has a temperature or any other problem," Gilchrist said of the dog.

Felix Omondi, 11, and his family, who live in the compound, have taken the dog in.

The dog, a tan short-haired mixed breed who was heavy

with milk from nursing, was possibly trying to care for the child because most of her puppies had died, Gilchrist said.

She looks a bit depressed? She's full of milk, aching to be a mom. All her puppies have died and now they've taken away her one last hope.

"*She looks a bit depressed?*" I'm saying to Betty, who is lying at my feet, curled up like a perfectly sturdy footstool. "They think she might have a . . . *temperature?*" I'm saying, irate and out of breath. "Can you believe this?"

"I can't believe it!" Betty says. "It's an outrage! It defies explanation! That poor lonely dog!"

Exactly. (And thank God someone around this joint understands me.) Get that dog a puppy. A kitten, a baby hamster, a little lizard that needs love, anything.

I can't, I suppose, help but see the world this way. Something magnificent happens in your life, and pretty soon you think it is the answer to every aching heart. You start seeing it here and there, repeating itself, you see it in the news stories you read and in the vacant eyes of some old chicken walking by. It becomes a song you'll never get out of your head so you might as well sing it.

Motherhood was my rescue. Motherhood.

acknowledgments

I wish to thank Alex and Anna and Sasha, my beloved little family, for providing me with more material than any author could ever hope for.

As always I am grateful to my agent, Andrew Blauner, for his tireless friendship and support, and to Kate Miciak, my editor at Bantam, for her patience, enthusiasm, and the trust with which she gives me such glorious room to roam. My thanks to the people of the English Department at the University of Pittsburgh, for the formative and essential part they've played all these years.

I wish to thank my sisters, Kristin, Claire, and Eileen, for all the lessons on how to be a mom. Finally, and once again, I thank my mother, whose example finds its way onto each page I write.

about the author

JEANNE MARIE LASKAS is a columnist for the *Washington Post Magazine*, where her "Significant Others" essays appear weekly. A *GQ* correspondent, she writes for numerous national magazines. She is the author of *The Balloon Lady and Other People I Know; We Remember; Fifty Acres and a Poodle;* and the award-winning *The Exact Same Moon*. A professor in the creative writing program at the University of Pittsburgh, she also writes the "My Life as a Mom" column for *Ladies' Home Journal*. She lives with her husband and two daughters at Sweetwater Farm in Scenery Hill, Pennsylvania.